What I Learned On The Way To The Scale

by Barbara Odom

TABLE OF CONTENTS

ACKNOWLEDGEMENTS

I'd like to give special appreciation to those who helped me through these valuable life lessons:

- Ultimately, the Holy Spirit Who was, and is, my Teacher. Without Him I could not learn or change any thing. He is the Strength of my life.

- To my sister Sharon Jantz who is my editor and encourager in the writing of this book.

- To my Husband, Tim, who has walked with me for 27 years in addition to my weight loss journey and the writing of this book. He's encouraged me even when I wanted to give up.

- To my daughter, Chelsee for encouraging me to eat foods not just low in calories, but high in health. And for her husband Paul that has helped train me in exercise.

- To my daughter, Lindsay for continually telling me that I could do it and for her husband Justin who played tennis with me daily while I visited with them.

- To my Weight Watcher lecturer, Dana, for her faithfulness to the men and women who show up week after week to hear a simple teaching regarding a difficult expedition.

- To my friends, family and church family who supported me with words of encouragement. Their words caused me to begin looking at myself differently so that I didn't just see the "fat" person I had seen for so many years.

FORWARD

How do we overcome ourselves? So often we place blame on anyone and everyone else for our own lack of willingness to obey (also called rebellion). "OUCH!" We say! "You've got me all wrong, I WANT to do the right thing, but I just CAN'T!"

In this very bold, frank and vulnerable book, you will find yourself identifying with the author again and again. No sugarcoating (forgive the pun) the truth here. Just real-life honesty.

As you read, you'll find that you no longer have a feeling of despair (an utter lack of hope). No longer will you feel beyond repair, correction or salvation. As I read I felt a small flicker of "well, maybe", and then the flicker was fanned into a flame that actually became HOPE.

HOPE is EXPECTATION WITH JOY!

Read this book with expectation. Permit the words and message of this book to penetrate the walls <u>you have surrounded yourself with</u>. Though this book disguises itself as lessons learned about weight loss; you will find it deals with every facet of your life. God's Grace is sufficient to transform all of us into worthy servants of Christ.

So, how do we overcome ourselves? "We overcome by the Blood of the Lamb and the Word of our testimony (Rev 12:11)."

We are forgiven, loved and disciplined by our Creator. Our Father is more than available, able and willing to walk beside us in any challenge or endeavor He asks us to accomplish. "As your day is, so shall your strength be." (Deut 33:25 KJV)

Readers, read with anticipation. Look up the scriptures, underline them, memorize them, repeat them to yourself when you're discouraged or tempted. Write them on sticky notes and place them EVERYWHERE!!!!

"Now, to He Who is able to do EXCEEDINGLY, ABUNDANTLY MORE, than we can ask or even think…. to Him be Glory…" (Eph 3:20 KJV)

Sharon Jantz

INTRODUCTION

In 2005 Hurricane Katrina devastated the states lining the Gulf of Mexico. Countless families were left homeless, businesses were destroyed, over 1300 people died and thousands are still unaccounted for. Some have named Hurricane Katrina the worst natural disaster in the United States since the San Francisco earthquake in 1906.

As I watched people seek refuge in stadiums, churches and auditoriums that were still standing, my heart yearned to help. Over the next several days my eyes were fixed on the darkness this nation was facing as I watched the national news coverage turn attention to the people who were stepping in to serve those in desperate need. Many searched for loved ones through water, mud, and even alligator beds for three days without stopping for sleep. I asked the Lord, "How can they search with such stamina?" and He gently said to me, "A healthy body has tremendous ability".

My husband and I pastor a wonderful church in Bullhead City, Arizona. The City is located right beside the Colorado River at the point where the Davis Dam and Hoover Dam, aka: Boulder Dam, create Lake Mohave. If either of these dams were to burst or be destroyed, our area would be devastated and flooded with water. I began asking myself "If disaster came to Bullhead City, would I have the stamina and endurance to help those in need? Would I be able to help myself? Do I have a healthy body?" In all honesty, I was neither healthy nor physically fit. "How would I be able to help people in need? How could the Holy Spirit use me as a tool if I was so physically unfit? How was that glorifying to God?" After all, the Word of God teaches us to glorify God in our body as well as our spirit in **1 Corinthians 6:20.** ***"For ye are bought with a price: therefore glorify God in your body, and in your spirit, which are God's."***

About the same time as Hurricane Katrina, I was fighting a physical problem that caused me extreme pain through my stomach, heart and chest area. Because of the ministry God had called me to I had studied healing extensively and had seen Jesus heal many precious people. I knew He had already paid a great price for my healing on the cross and I also knew if Jesus bore my sickness and disease I didn't need to bear it. But I was definitely experiencing symptoms in my body of a major problem and yet Jesus said in **Matthew 8:17** ***"That it might be fulfilled which was spoken by Isaiah the prophet, saying, Himself took our infirmities, and bore our sicknesses."***

There was one more 'eye-opener' that brought me to the valley of decision. I had just returned from a mission trip to Jamaica with Foursquare Youth Outreach to which I took six teens from our church to a camp in Jamaica where we worked side by side with Caribbean churches and teenagers and then shared time in the presence of the Lord as we worshipped Him together. I loved it, with one exception; I was not physically in shape. To make things worse, I had broken my little toe the day before we left the U.S. to travel to Jamaica.

While on our mission we walked up and down hills and worked hard in the extreme humid heat. One day in particular, we were walking to the river. Another chaperone from a Foursquare Church in Oregon was walking with me and besides the limp due to my broken toe; my legs were shaking uncontrollably as we walked down hill. I felt as if my legs were going to give out, so periodically I stopped to rest. My friend asked if I wanted to go back to the dorm but I refused to miss out on anything, so I continued in my shaky state.

I had offered myself as a vessel to the Lord, willing to go anywhere for Him and preach the Gospel. However, I found myself in a position that I was not physically fit. Had I disqualified myself for His service? There were three desires of my heart:

(1) I wanted to be physically prepared to help people in disaster;

(2) I needed healing in my body; and,

(3) I wanted to be physically fit in order to ably reach out to the world with the Gospel.

The Truth was, God was asking me to glorify Him with my body. That meant, I had to take control and after 20+ years, that would not be an easy task.

Over many years I had tried to lose weight and like many others, I failed over and over again. I cried out to the Lord, "God, don't ask me to do this because I can't!" Following that cry I used excuse after excuse of why I couldn't succeed at what God was asking me to do until I realized that all the excuses I used were really just that, empty excuses. You see, God is not unjust. He will not ask us to do what He won't help us to accomplish and so He, the Holy Spirit, reminded me of something that would give me His grace and ability, to begin this journey. It's found in **Deuteronomy 30:14, 19-20** *(Amplified) "But the Word is very near you, in your mouth and in your mind and in your heart, so that you can do it…I call heaven and earth to witness this day against you that I have set before you life and death, the blessings and the curses; therefore choose life, that you and your descendants may live. And may you love the Lord your God, obey His voice, and cling to Him. For He is your life and the length of your days"*.

The Holy Spirit is a brilliant Teacher. Several things stood out to me in the previous verses and I personalized them since this Bible is God speaking to *me* (and you as well).

- "<u>Barbara</u> can do it"

- "<u>God set before Barbara</u> life and death…<u>Barbara</u> choose life"
- <u>If Barbara</u> chooses life "<u>Barbara and her children will live</u>"
- "Love God, obey and <u>cling</u> to Him"
- "<u>He (alone) is the length of Barbara's days</u>".

Do you see that? We can depend on Jesus. He's Trustworthy and Faithful. Isn't His Word so good? You see, the Word of God changes people and changed people change the situations around them. Did I have a lot of weight to lose? Yes! Were there a lot of excuses to be unveiled and lessons to be learned? Of course there were. **<u>But the journey is not greater than His grace.</u>**

Chapter One

"IT'S NOT MY FAULT"

When my oldest daughter had her first daughter she said to me, "I'm gonna lose weight right after I have this baby because I'm *not* going to have a big stomach". Lightheartedly my response was, "I said that, too". Then I began to think of all the women in my family so I continued, "In fact, my mother said that, and her mother, and her mother". You see, I was not taking the blame for my weight being out of control. I didn't think it was my fault. In fact, it must be hereditary and although I didn't want my daughter to inherit this trait I thought it might be possible. "It's in the genes dear". Thank God she didn't listen to me because I was way off. Through dedication and hard work she did lose the weight and continues to keep her body in control through exercise and healthy eating. However, my experience had been different.

As a child I never experienced a weight problem. Nevertheless, when I became a teenager I was a little larger than some girls by about 20 lbs, but not what you would consider to be obese. I was always watching my weight, learning new exercises and looking for that "magic something" that would make me thin for the rest of my life. However my 'problem', so I assumed, was when my family would bring out the Pepsi and chips after church, it was just too much temptation for me to resist. So I summed it up as "It's not my fault", it's my parents fault.

For five months I attended what is now known as Vanguard University in Orange County California and ate in the cafeteria. I discovered on my own, however, where the drive through donut shops were and learned that I could eat 3 donuts in the car on the way back to the dorm and then have only one in front of my roommate so she didn't think I was over-eating. Of course, if anyone noticed I was putting on a few extra pounds they would logically assume it was the result of eating the starchy commercial meals prepared in the cafeteria. Because you see, "it wasn't my fault."

I married a wonderful and patient man that was raised with good southern cookin', and since I liked southern eatin' as much as he did we fried everything we could and the rest of our food was full of sugar and flour. Nothing whole grain, green or fruity about it. I even kept a jar of grease on the stove like our ancestors because I would need that grease the next time I cooked. I know its grotesque and it's not easy for me to admit these things but it's the truth. A few more pounds came on as a result of my "good cookin'" and I was on my way to not losing weight but <u>losing control</u>. After all, "It wasn't really my fault." If my husband didn't like such good cookin', *then* I could lose weight.

Immediately after my first baby was born I returned to my weight before pregnancy, which was on this 5'7" frame 180 lbs, and then became pregnant with my second child. After she was born I had a friend that introduced me to diet pills prescribed by what we called the "diet doctor" and I lost more weight than I could've imagined at the time and ended up wearing a size 5 to 7.

That seemed like an easy victory but I realized it was really no victory at all. I didn't really do anything to win that fight. I just simply took the pill and didn't eat because I didn't feel like eating and I soon learned that those "diet pills" cause horrendous damage both physically and emotionally. Of course, when I stopped taking the pills the weight came back on because I had not made any permanent changes in being in control of what I ate, and why I ate. In fact, I could barely eat but my weight continued to climb. But, "it wasn't my fault." "Those pills have messed up my metabolism," I said, and my doctor concurred with my assessment. So that was my excuse to gain weight. In my perception, it had nothing to do with the fact that I was eating too much of the wrong foods for all the wrong reasons.

The Holy Spirit tried to help me in several ways. In 1986 I was listening to one of my Bible School instructors teach on taking care of our temple. I walked out of that class knowing that what he said was the truth but I was so angry. I reasoned, "He just doesn't understand, this isn't my fault. My metabolism just doesn't work as fast as others." So I continued in my stubborn, rebellious, unlearned state and my weight continued to soar.

In 1990 we went on staff at a church in Southern California where the pastor's wife was beautiful and a size 2. In 1995, after reaching my top weight of 260 lbs and a size 24, I decided that since this "isn't my fault" I must have a medical problem. The doctor asked me questions like, "Are you tired a lot? Have you been more hungry than usual?" "Well, yes, I am tired a lot and, yes, I am hungry all the time. I knew it! It's not my fault." She ran some blood tests and the results showed that I had an under-active thyroid. (By the way, I received healing in my thyroid gland in 1997).

I had blamed family, husband, school administration, children, medical professionals, and personal metabolism and glands. Now came the big one. My rationale was, "God must want me to be big. After all, He made me and loves me just the way I am, so why am I even trying to change that." After all, "It's not my fault, it's His". This must be God's will for me.

Was I listening to myself? I was blaming God for all the times that I stuffed my face just because I was bored or stressed and not hungry at all. I was blaming God for gaining weight because I chose to eat the whole bag of potato chips, or the bag of Oreo cookies my husband had bought so we could have a cookie or two (or a dozen), when the children went to bed. What about the ½ dozen donuts I would buy at the drive through and eat them that day then buy another ½ dozen the next day? Was it in God's will for me to eat all that food? Did I really talk to Him about it and listen to what He had to say? If it was not my fault, then did God force feed me? If it's His plan to keep me big and His will that I'm overweight, then I must be doing the will of God when I'm over indulging in all these foods that are unhealthy for my body.

I was messed up in my thinking and I knew I needed the grace of God because this was not anyone's fault but my own. *I* had lost control of my eating and *I* would have to regain it.

I Needed Grace for the Pace

Many years would pass because of my refusal to yield to God in this area of my life. I would lose some and gain some. For years I fluctuated between 240 and 250 lbs. And then the day came in 2005 when I would have to make a choice. You see God has given us a choice. He said in **Deuteronomy**

30:19 *(NLT) "Today I have given you the choice between life and death, between blessings and curses. I call on heaven and earth to witness the choice you make. Oh, that you would choose life, that you and your descendants might live!"*

From this verse I knew that if I were to take the first step and choose life, God would meet me there and give me the grace to go through this journey. It wouldn't happen overnight but if I would trust Him, it would eventually happen. So I admitted I needed help. I had experienced God's grace in other areas of my life and it was good, so good. However, in this area, I didn't even know where to begin. I must admit, I needed God's grace to help me.

According to Webster's dictionary grace is "unmerited divine assistance given man for his sanctification of virtue coming from God". We didn't earn or even deserve His assistance but He would give it to us anyway. That's grace. In Webster's 1828 dictionary one of the definitions is "Favorable influence of God; in renewing the heart and restraining from sin". I need God's favorable influence on me and Paul said in **II Corinthians 12:9 that "*God's grace is sufficient for me…*". The Amplified Bible says "*…My grace is enough for you*".**

The Grace of God was the <u>answer</u> the Holy Spirit was leading me to. It was the lesson I was learning on the way to the scale. So if it's grace, God's divine assistance, God's influence that I need, then how do

I get more because I was anticipating needing a lot of it. The Holy Spirit revealed the answer to me, but if you're not ready to hear it, read no further.

<u>WARNING: YOU MAY NOT LIKE WHAT YOU READ!</u>

1 Peter 5:5
"…for God resisteth the proud, and giveth grace to the humble."

1 Peter 5:5 *in the Amplified version says,*
"For God sets Himself against the proud
(the insolent, the overbearing, the disdainful, the
presumptuous, the boastful)--[and He opposes,
frustrates, and defeats them],
but gives grace (favor, blessing) to the
humble."

God gives grace to the humble. In fact, He sets Himself *against* the proud. "You mean I have a pride problem and God has set Himself against me?" It was my pride that blamed everyone else for my problem. It was my pride that said it couldn't possibly be *my* fault. But the truth was, if I would deal with the sin of my pride and humble myself before the Lord accepting responsibility for what I alone had done, AND, if I would deal with my pride; then this trip to the scale would be different and this passage of lessons would help me in every area of my life.

I knew other people that were prideful but that did not describe me, so I thought. Even though under the anointing and help of the Holy Spirit, I could preach and teach His Word, I was rather quiet and reserved for the most part. But God was now telling me that I was full of pride.

Pride is just as much sin as anything else and it must be dealt with. We must repent and run in the opposite direction of sin, in my case that was pride. Pride was defiling me. Me, a minister of the Gospel of Jesus Christ! But Jesus said in **Mark 7:20-23 (New Living Translation)** ***"It is the thought-life that defiles you. For from within, out of a person's heart, come evil thoughts, sexual immorality, theft, murder, adultery, greed, wickedness, deceit, eagerness for lustful pleasure, envy, slander, <u>pride</u>, and foolishness."***

Pride Was My Problem

The thing that was stopping me from losing weight was <u>manifested on the inside</u> not on the outside. It was my thought-life that was defiling me. From within me came pride that caused me to blame everyone else for my circumstance. Just as the Psalmist had written: **Psalm 73:6** ***"Pride compassed me about as a chain"***.

You see a chain keeps a body from moving, going and doing as you would please and that's what pride was doing to me. I was bound by a chain of pride, blaming everyone else for things that I had brought on myself. I had the choice all along. It wasn't anyone's fault but *mine* and if I would accept that, the chain of pride would be broken.

I was so full of pride that I had refused advice from those that God, unknowingly to me, had put in my life over and over throughout the years. When the advice was given to me it would seem as if I were receiving but after a few days I would return to my prideful state and begin to quarrel about why their advice would not work for me. God says in **Proverbs 13:10 (New International Version) *"Pride only breeds quarrels, but wisdom is found in those who take advice."***

The day came when I was desperate to hear the Truth and if I were to lose the weight I so desired to lose and get physically fit, I would need the grace of God to do it. So there was only one thing to do. Humble myself, repent and yield to the Lord and His grace.

After spending time in prayer, asking the Lord where to begin, He led me to attend Weight Watchers meetings. They are well balanced and easy to understand. *Now that's what He instructed <u>me</u> to do – you listen to what He instructs YOU to do!* This was the fourth time I had joined Weight Watchers, the first being in 1978, and I had lost a little weight each time but never finished my course, let alone with joy. This program offers tools that will help you look at food differently and teach you how to eat, why to eat and how to get your body moving. But if you don't use those tools your chances of losing weight are reduced. These are practical proven steps to nutrition and fitness. My problem in the past had been I didn't follow the steps and then I would say "the program doesn't work". Pride says "I'm not really getting anything out of the meeting". But if you're determined to learn, you can follow the Spirit of Truth and He'll help you find a lesson in every lecture. This time I was determined that it would be different for me, this time, I desired to *"finish my course with joy"* **(Acts 20:24).**

I would soon find out that the lessons on the way to scale would carry over into every area of my life as *"I am being changed into His image, from glory to glory even by the Spirit of the Lord"* **(II Corinthians 3:18).** Oh how I desired to bring glory to the Lord in my body, but there were more excuses to confront that I had told myself for years and more lessons to be learned. This would not happen overnight. And sometimes I wondered if it would really happen at all?

Chapter Two

THE FEAR OF FAILURE

Because of the physical problems I had been facing if I didn't lose weight I was facing surgery. In fact my doctor had put me on a liquid diet for several weeks to help with the pain I was experiencing when I was eating. The pain subsided partially and I did lose 14 lbs, but I knew I couldn't live like that for the rest of my life. So my choice was to pay the fees that Weight Watchers receives for their services or pay for the surgery. I opted for Weight Watchers.

October 3, 2005 I stood in line at my first meeting trying to decide if I should just pay the registration fee and then the weekly dues or if I should take the deal where I pay for 5 weeks and save a little bit of money. What if I work on this a couple of days and give up? What if I work on this and don't lose any weight? What if I end up wasting my money? The next question was **"<u>WHAT IF I FAIL?</u>"**

I reasoned it through my limited wisdom and thought, "I'll join for 5 weeks and save money. I'll work at it hard for 5 weeks, but if it doesn't do anything for me, then I'll quit". Notice I said "it." I was starting off with a system to blame anyone but me.

At the time I thought I was making a wise decision but in actuality I was leaving room to give myself permission to fail or permission to quit and neither choice was an option the Lord had given me.

After registering I went to my seat and my thoughts went back to something a friend said to me in 1984. This friend was Neva Coyle who has authored many books including <u>Free to Be Thin</u>. She shared with me that when she began to lose weight she told the Lord she was going to do this for Him. She said that He gently corrected her and said "No, I'm going to do this for you". Now I was sitting in this Methodist Church fellowship hall on a cold chair and my question to the Holy Spirit was "will you do this for me too?" As bold as I may appear to others, emotionally I was afraid I was going to fail.

By the grace of God, I lost 11 lbs during those first five weeks and that achievement helped me to believe that this time I might be able to reach my goal. But another great challenge was coming.

Friends and Family

Before I made the decision to join Weight Watchers I had told only a few people that I was thinking about it and the responses were not very favorable. The comments didn't help but I was in so much need of a change I had to try one more time. Comments such as "All you have to do is work-out". "I don't know how you have that kind of money to go to those meetings". Each one had their own idea of what it would, or would not, take for me to lose weight. I'm sure everyone had good intentions, but it wasn't what the Holy Spirit was leading me to do. So I had decided to not tell anyone else and if the weight began to come off then I would share what I was doing.

Two weeks after I began the Weight Watchers meetings, our church camp meeting/Revival that we host annually began. At camp meeting we have at least three guest speakers come, their spouses, as well as out of town guests that come to receive from the Lord. Several of the ministers and people that come are very good friends of ours and return for these meetings every year. In addition to my friends coming I had another dilemma.

We have extremely gifted cooks in our church that provide lunch and dinner for all of our ministers during the whole week. Our usual schedule is that we eat after the morning meetings about 1:00 p.m. and then again after church, late at night, about 10:00 p.m. I had done so well for two weeks and I had a decision to make. My choices were:

(1) Because I wanted this to be my secret I could decide to count my points silently;

(2) when everyone came to my house after

church I could excuse myself and go to bed; or

(3) I could have a week of feasting and begin again when everyone was gone.

If I chose option #2, that would be rude. If I chose option #3, I would gain all the weight back that I had worked so hard to lose and may not return to eating right again. So my only choice was option #1. I would choose to not tell anyone and count my points silently. But it didn't work out the way I had intended.

Everyone sat at the large dinner table and filled his or her plates with food that gave off a breathtaking home cookin' aroma. The steam from the freshly cooked food flowed upward just close enough to the nose to make anyone crave more. My plate was the exception. I filled it with just enough food for me, watching every portion, but it was very noticeable that it wasn't a normal "American" helping. After all, most homes and restaurants give you enough food on a plate for two to three people.

I got through the first afternoon meal without any-one saying anything but now we had the late night meal to conquer. Eating late at night was something I was trying to avoid, but this week would have to be an exception. I've read articles in magazines and heard physicians and nutritionists alike say that you should not eat 2-3 hours before going to bed, so I was endeavoring to incorporate that in my new eat-ing habits.

Everyone arrived at my home and we sat down to eat. Someone noticed that I wasn't eating much and asked if I was all right. "Uh-oh, here's the big question", I thought. "What am I going to say? I can't lie to them so what can I say? What answer do I give them and still keep my secret? If I tell them my secret what will their response be"? Not only did I have a fear of failure, but I had a fear of rejection and criticism. I was afraid that my closest friends were going to reject me. But why would they? One couple had known me since 1986. Another had known me since 1996 and still my other friends had known me since 1998. There was only one minister there that I had just recently met, but why would any one of my closest friends criticize me?

I took a chance. "Well, I just joined Weight Watchers…I don't know if it's going to work or not, but I've lost a few pounds already". Did you notice that? I continued to leave room for rejection. Just in case they were more spiritual and had a reason why I should not be doing this I could have a place to agree. I looked at each face in hopes that someone would side with me and one by one they began to respond.

"I know someone that did Weight Watchers and lost 35 lbs". "We're so proud of you, Barbara". "That's the best thing you could have done". "Don't they give each food a point value?" These were the responses I received, but they were more than statements and questions. They were responses of love and acceptance for me.

Its amazing what words of love and affirmation can do. You never quite know where people are at and how the Lord is working in their lives. But just a few simple words can help someone else, when those words are given in love.

I began to tell them how the point system worked and they all began amazingly to look at their plates and count their own points. From that moment on, we had fun while we all counted points all week, even points for desserts, and when I returned to weigh in the following week I had still lost 3.8 lbs.

The fear of failure has stopped people from reaching dreams and goals that they have envisioned for many years. What if we really did believe that *with* God, nothing was impossible? What if we knew that we could tell anyone anything and no matter what their responses were we could still achieve our goals?

Trust your friends and family. I think you'll be pleasantly surprised that they are on your side. And in the few cases that they're not, remember God is. He said in **Psalm 118:6** ***"The LORD is on my side; I will not fear: what can man do unto me?"*** in the New Living Translation it reads like this, ***"The LORD is for me, so I will not be afraid. What can mere mortals do to me?"*** Another verse that confirms this Truth is **Psalm 56:9** ***"...this I know; for***

God is for me." Then over in the New Testament the Lord repeats Himself when He says in **Romans 8:31** *"What shall we then say to these things? If God be for us, who can be against us?"*

How can we fail with God on our side? If we truly trust Him, *and* obey His leading, failure is not an option because *"God <u>always</u> causes us to triumph in Christ" (2 Cor 2:14).* You might have to tell yourself the truth several times before you believe it. But if there were a possibility that God really is for you, then wouldn't you rather stand in faith believing that God's Word will come to pass than believe the lies of the enemy? Fear is one of those lies.

Fear

One of my favorite verses is **II Timothy 1:7** *"For God hath not given us the spirit of fear; but of power, and of love, and of a sound mind."* It's easy to memorize and it would do us all good to hide this Word in our heart so that the Holy Spirit can bring it back to our memory as we need it.

The Greek word for fear in this verse is "deilia" which when translated means timidity, fearfulness, and cowardice. Do you see it? God has not given Barbara, (or fill your own name in there) a spirit of timidity, fearfulness, and cowardice.

The Amplified Bible makes it real clear when translating **II Timothy 1:7** *"For God did not give us a spirit of timidity (of cowardice, of craven and cringing and fawning fear), but [He has given us a* *spirit] of power and of love and of a calm and well-balanced mind and discipline and self-control."*

My problem is not necessarily fear of the enemy because I know my authority over him. Jesus said in **Luke 10:19** *"Behold, I give unto you power (authority) to tread on serpents and scorpions, and over all the power (ability) of the enemy: and nothing shall by any means hurt you."*

However, notice the Amplified version of II Timothy 1:7 says that some of the tools He gave us was discipline and self-control. *That* was my problem? Discipline and self-control? Why? Did I believe the lies of the devil more than I believed God? That's not easy for me to say because I'm a woman of the Word. I preach the Gospel and have led people to the Lord and have seen people healed of bodily ailments. But this is where I was, emotionally and physically, and to say anything less would be dishonest.

Failure had become more possible and probable to me than discipline and self-control. Why? I know why. I had carried around an extra 100 lbs for over 20 years, and had tried numerous times to lose that excess weight but all I did was fail and fail again. This time, am I going to believe God's Word or the devil's lies?

I believe God's Word more than anything else. His Word is forever Truth. I don't walk by my physical senses but by faith. Faith in what? Faith in a God that is Faithful to His every Word. If **we**

"Commit our way to the Lord; trust also in Him; He shall bring it to pass". **(Psalm 37:5).** It was time for me to really commit *this* area of my life to the Lord. Was I ready to do what it takes? Was I willing to pay the price?

Commitment

The Hebrew word for commit in **Psalm 37:5** is to "roll". **The Amplified Bible** says

"Commit your way to the Lord [roll and repose each care of your load on Him]…".

Rick Renner, a modern-day Greek Scholar tells us in the New Testament the Greek word for commit is "paradidomi", a compound of the words "para" and "didomi". The word "para" means "alongside and carries the idea of coming close alongside to someone or to some object". The word "didomi" means "to give". When compounded together, it presents the idea of "entrusting something to someone". The prefix "para" suggests that "this is someone to whom you have drawn very close". It can be translated "to commit, to yield…or to hand something over to someone else". (Renner: page 234)

This was what I needed to do. I needed to hand my problem of excess weight and all the issues that caused me to get like this, over to the Lord. Commit myself to Him; just hand my thoughts, my actions, and my weaknesses over to Him.

We have all read or heard about people that committed themselves to others and nothing could move them. They were in it for the long haul. Families that stuck together through tragedy and war, in the good times and perilous times. Marriages that could not be torn apart no matter what, and sons that took over the family business when their father could no longer work. What caused these people to not be moved? Commitment.

Webster's 1828 dictionary defines commit as "to give in trust; to put into the hands of another". I was at a place that I would have to put my life in the hands of my Lord and Savior, Jesus Christ. I had given my life to Him as a child, and then rededicated myself to Him many times throughout my life. But I found myself once again putting my very existence into His hands and realizing that I'll be doing this throughout my time here on earth. He's not finished with me and I haven't "arrived". So whatever He tells me to do, I must do it. Not just *know* I need to do it, but really do it.

It's one thing to read the Word, but it's another thing to *do* the Word. We know this is true just from the standpoint of salvation. Just because you know *about* Jesus doesn't mean you know Him. You can receive Him into your life as your personal Lord and Savior by **believing that God raised Jesus from the dead and confessing Jesus as Lord (Romans 10:9-10).** But then you get to *know* Him by reading His Word, talking with Him, and going to church to develop and grow as a Christian and be connected to the Body of Christ. But you wouldn't really *know* Him if you stopped at the sinners' prayer and returned to a life of sin because "faith without works is dead".

Although it's not our works that save us but faith in the Blood of Jesus to cleanse us of all sin (**Ephesians 2:8-9**), the Bible tells us more in **James 2:20-24 (NLT)** *"...faith that does not result in good deeds is useless? Don't you remember that our ancestor Abraham was declared right with God because of what he did when he offered his son Isaac on the altar? You see, he was trusting God so much that he was willing to do whatever God told him to do. His faith was made complete by what he did — by his actions. And so it happened just as the Scriptures say: "Abraham believed God, so God declared him to be righteous." He was even called "the friend of God." So you see, we are made right with God by what we do, not by faith alone."*

It's one thing to read the Word, but another thing to do the Word. **James 1:22 *"But be ye doers of the word, and not hearers only, deceiving your own selves."*** So it is with natural things as well as spiritual. Once I committed my eating habits and choices to the Lord, *doing* what He instructed me to do, I was on my way to the winners' circle.

One thing He instructed me to do was become teachable in this area. I must allow someone to speak the truth to me in love and help me change the way I respond to food. There was a lot I had to learn and the only way I was going to learn was if I were to listen, <u>really</u> listen.

The first night I showed up for Weight Watchers I saw this beautiful, thin, young woman giving the lecture. Her voice was soft and quiet and hard to be heard over the noise in a room with tile floors, several windows and lots of people. My first thought was "She's not that motivating". But the Lord didn't ask me to come and judge the lecturer, He asked me to come and learn. That meant I had to listen. This leader has since become one of my favorite lecturers. I don't know if she became a better speaker or if I became a better listener, but I know the meetings helped me to succeed.

Had I not obeyed the Lord in the area of commitment I can guarantee you I would not have lost over 100lbs. Fear of failure is not a problem. If I commit to do what God has asked me to do, I cannot fail because God will not fail me. ***"…for He [God] Himself has said, I will not in any way fail you nor give you up nor leave you without support. [I will] not,[I will] not, [I will] not in any degree leave you helpless nor forsake you nor let [you] down (relax My hold on you)! [Assuredly not!]*** **(Hebrews 13:5 AMP).**

Now that you're committed to do what He asks you to do you can line your words up to faith-filled words or fear-filled words. What you say and believe will determine your results.

Fear or Faith?

Everyday we choose to speak words of fear or faith. If you really listen to yourself you will be amazed at what you say and what you really believe. To remain committed I have to make certain that I say what God says. Because when God changes our heart, He changes our mouth. ***"Out of the abundance of the heart the mouth speaks"*** **(Luke 6:45).**

When things don't seem to be going right you can choose to agree or disagree but the result will be life or death to that situation. For example, when your emotions are trying to control you and tell you that you need to "eat something to feel better" and you think a Cinnabon would take care of everything, you have to make a choice. Since ***"Death and life are in the power of the tongue and they that love it shall eat the fruit thereof"*** **(Proverbs 18:21);** you might want to choose to say "I stand on the Word of God and ***"In patience, possess my soul"*** **(Luke 21:19).** [Just a side note here, your soul is your mind, will and emotions]. Continue to say, I decide right now that I'm going to make a healthy choice because my *body belongs to the Lord and He will get glory in this body"*. Then get up and take a walk, or work out, play a game with your family, or go out to the patio to read your Bible and pray, just get your body busy and get out of the house.

You can definitely control yourself with what you say. According **to James 3:2 *"We all make many mistakes, but those who control their tongues can also control themselves in every other way."* NLT**

Why do we think that tomorrow will be different if we do the same thing we've always done? Our future can be different, if we're willing to change today.

It's time to change what we say, and in so doing change what we have. This takes exercising self-control and isn't it wonderful that the Holy Spirit brought that with Him, this fruit, when He came to live permanently in us? Shouldn't we begin to develop this fruit of self-control, and walk in it to the best of our ability if we're going to bring glory to God in our bodies?

The Lord was preparing me for another lesson on the way to the scale. A lesson that was not easy, but oh so necessary.

Chapter Three

I CAN'T HELP IT!

My paternal grandparents were Texans, and a common expression they used (and passed down to my family) was, "Cain't Hep It!" When the phrase was used you knew something "couldn't be helped" and the consequences were out of anyone's control and no one would try to change it.

As I overate my way into obesity I adapted the "cain't hep it" concept. Many times I opened a bag of chips, ate the whole bag and then said "Well, cain't hep' it". But the truth was, this problem <u>was</u> <u>not</u> beyond my control.

Lack of self-control reveals itself in many different ways. When you speed every time you get behind the wheel, you lack self-control. When you have sex outside of the marriage covenant, you lack self-control. When you strive with others habitually you lack self-control. When you spend multiple hours a day in front of the television, surfing the internet or playing electronic games you lack self-control. For me, lack of self-control was manifesting itself in my eating habits.

You know you lack self-control when any of the following happen:

- You open a bag of chips and can't stop eating until the last one is gone.
- You overeat and feel "stuffed" at Thanksgiving dinner but find you're putting leftover food in your mouth as you clean up the kitchen.
- You order a half dozen donuts and eat three of them on the way home.
- You sit in front of the television and eat a whole quart of ice cream in one sitting.
- You eat another piece of cake every time you walk past the cake pan.
- You put another cookie in your mouth without even thinking about it.
- You can't go one week without eating your favorite food.

If you experience any of these symptoms you may have a lack of self-control.

Can you imagine a world with entirely no self-control? A society of people that have the opinion of I can do anything I want simply because I feel like it? Talk shows make millions exploiting this fact everyday. People having sex with whomever they choose, without caring about the consequences.

Others stealing, lying, stirring up strife, abusing themselves (and others) with uncontrolled anger, alcohol, drugs and food. The list could go on and on. This is a symptom of the "me" generation.

In their book <u>Telling Yourself the Truth</u>, William Backus and Marie Chapian list a few reasons people use when making excuses for their lack of self-control.

> "There are lies people tell themselves when making excuses. You may have said them yourself. "If you want something you should have it – no matter what". "To be uncomfortable or frustrated is intolerable, so avoid distress at all costs". "You cannot control your strong desires. They are "needs" and they must be satisfied. Any time you have to spend being frustrated or ungratified is unendurable". "You can't fight your fleshly desires. They're much too strong". "You can't quit because you're much too weak. And besides, even though X is bad for you it meets your need for gratification". "You have rights. You're entitled to inflict your demands on others." (Backus: pages 81-82)

What has happened to us? Is this epidemic of self-centeredness only in America? Many years ago it was important to a family that their children develop self-control, and so discipline was enforced, obedience was expected, relating to authority was taught, truthfulness was anticipated, compassion was learned, attentiveness was called for and discretion was trained even to the youngest child.

However, when you study history, the turning point seems to be the era when men went off to war and women were forced to work, the result was children were left alone to rear themselves. Often times the oldest children were placed in charge but if they were off at college, work, or war themselves, children were raising children. And so we had the first "teenagers" after WWI and lack of self-control was their game.

These teenagers became adults and brought their philosophies with them. Others picked up on this idea of "I don't have to do anything I don't want to do" and created a society of self-indulgence, self-proclamation, and lack of self-control.

The self-control that we speak of is found in **Galatians 5:22-24 (NIV)** *"But the fruit of the Spirit is love, joy, peace, patience, kindness, goodness, faithfulness, gentleness and self-control. Against such things there is no law."*

The Word self-control is the word temperance in the King James Version. This word temperance is the Greek word (Strongs NT:1466) egkrateia which means self-control. This word egkrateia comes from the Greek word (Strongs NT:1468) egkrates which means "strong in a thing (masterful), self-controlled (in appetite, etc.)".

The Merriam-Webster Dictionary says self-control is *"restraint exercised over one's own impulses, emotions, or desires."*

Self-control is one of the Fruit of the Spirit and when the Holy Spirit comes in to our human spirit to take up residence He brings self-control with Him. So what's the problem?

You must first understand that when you accept Jesus as your Lord and Savior you become a new man. **II Corinthians 5:17 (KJV) says "Therefore if any man be in Christ, he is a new creature: old things are passed away; behold, all things are become new."** Then in **Ephesians 4:24 (KJV) God says "...ye put on the new man, which after God is created in righteousness and true holiness."**

Why do we lack in the area of self-control if this power was deposited into us at the new birth and why is it such a struggle to control ourselves when it comes to relating to and obeying authority, telling the truth, showing compassion, paying attention to detail, being discrete, or even controlling our appetite?

Quoting Walter Martinez from his book <u>Building Better Relationships</u> he states:

> One reason we lack self-control is because we view ourselves as the old man rather than the new. Our "bad experiences" help to create an old man mentality. The difference between the old man and the new man

is the old man embraces feelings of failure and defeat. The new man is an overcomer and embraces victory. The old man allows his feelings to govern him, thus he embraces his feelings and wears them like a badge of courage and honor for the world to see. The new man embraces the truth of God's Word and allows only those feelings that can be produced through his faith in God. The new man's experiences are no different than the old man, but his faith in God changes his perspective. (Martinez: 25).

You will notice in **Galatians 5:22-24** that one of the fruit of the Spirit is self-control and the Holy Spirit did not call it "God-control". God is sovereign, meaning He is in control. But let's look at this. If He were in control of everything, and everyone at all times, then everyone would be saved because **I Timothy 2:4-6 *(NLT)* says *"…for He (God) wants everyone to be saved and to understand the truth. For there is only one God and one Mediator who can reconcile God and people. He is the man Christ Jesus. He gave his life to purchase freedom for everyone."***

The fact is Jesus did give His life to pay for our sins so that we could have eternal life. So if God is totally sovereign, or in control of everything, wouldn't He have his way in the salvation of mankind? Of course not. He wants us to love Him because we *choose* to love Him. He's given us a free will to choose life.

The outcome and sometimes consequence is, we are in control of some things.

One reason the earth is in such a mess is found in **Psalm 115:16** *"The heaven, even the heavens, are the LORD's: but the earth hath he given to the children of men."* The unregenerate man has made a mess of things on this earth. But if you have made Jesus your Lord, He has returned to you authority and dominion over your domain. Things can, and should, be different where you have authority.

The Apostle Paul said in **I Corinthians 9:27** *"But I keep under my body, and (I) bring it into subjection: lest that by any means, when I have preached to others, I myself should be a castaway.*

The Living Bible translates this verse like this *"Like an athlete I punish my body, treating it roughly, training it to do what it should, not what it wants to…"*. Other translations say *"I discipline my body…"*

God did not make Paul discipline his body. Paul said "…*I 'discipline' my body…training it to do what it should, not what it wants to"*. Paul was in control over his own body and so are we. If I really believed God was in control of everything I ate then I would have to say that He ordained every cookie I put in my mouth. From the first to the fifteenth. But He didn't *make* me eat the cookie and He didn't *make* me stop eating the cookies. I was in control of that and I have to admit, I lacked control.

If you've ever had a child that had an extreme weight problem you know what they need to do and you teach them and encourage them to eat right, eat smaller portions and exercise. But you can't do it for them. You might run along side them, but you cannot run for them. In the same way, with the encouragement of the Holy Spirit, **you** will have to rule your body & flesh with self-control. Don't let your body rule you.

How can I help it? How can I rule my body and bodily desires? How can I get in control?

Jesus has done everything He is going to do in redemption. He died once and for all. **Hebrews 10:11-12 *(NLT) "Under the old covenant, the priest stands before the altar day after day, offering sacrifices that can never take away sins. But our High Priest (Jesus) offered Himself to God as one sacrifice for sins, good for all time."***

In His death and resurrection He gave you authority to be an overcomer in *this* life. He sent the Holy Spirit to live in you to be your *"…Comforter (Counselor, Helper, Intercessor, Advocate, Strengthener, Standby)…"* **(John 14:26)**. He will teach you and tell you what you need to do, but <u>He won't do it for you</u>.

So, if I'm an overcomer why do I have so many problems in this area? You must first realize **<u>your flesh is an enemy of your spirit – it is NEVER your friend!</u>** (Thompson: page 119)

So walk smart because your flesh and spirit war against each other. **Galatians 5:17 (NAS)** says ***"For the flesh sets its desire against the spirit, and the spirit against the flesh; for these are in opposition to one another, so that you may not do the things that you please"***.

The War In You

There is a war going on and it's inside of you. 1 Thessalonians 5:23 tells us that we are a three part being - spirit, soul and body.

- Your **spirit** is the real you, the inward man, the part of your being that the Spirit of the Living God comes to indwell when you invite Him in. This is also the part of you that will live forever.

- Your **soul** is your mind, will and emotions.

- You live in a **body.** Without a body made of skin, blood, vital organs and bones you could not live on this earth.

Our <u>soul</u> (mind, will, emotions) and our <u>physical body</u> make up our flesh. Our flesh (soul/body) continually wars against our spirit. The flesh is trying to get you to do things you shouldn't and not to do things you should. The following passage of Scripture is very interesting. The writer, Paul, is describing the war that goes on between the spirit and the flesh. The passage can be confusing, so let's break it down. To help differentiate between the spirit and flesh I have added the words in parentheses.

Rom 7:15-19 *"For that which I (flesh) do I (spirit) allow not: for what I (spirit) would, that do I (flesh) not; but what I (spirit) hate, that do I (flesh). If then I (flesh) do that which I (spirit) would not, I (flesh) consent unto the law that it is good. Now then it is no more I (flesh) that do it, but sin that dwelleth in me. For I (spirit) know that in me (that is, in my flesh,) dwelleth no good thing: for to will is present with me; but how to perform that which is good I (spirit) find not. For the good that I (spirit) would I (flesh) do not: but the evil which I (spirit) would not, that I (flesh) do."*

Notice how the Apostle Paul's flesh and spirit are constantly at odds with one another. Our flesh continually tries to convince our spirit what we should and should not do. However, our spirit should rule and reign over our flesh. And we do that by walking IN the Spirit.

The only way to make sure that the flesh doesn't win this war that is being waged inside us every day of our lives is found in the following verse. **Galatians 5:16 (NAS)** *"But I say, walk by the Spirit, and you will not carry out the desire of the flesh"*.

What does it mean to walk by the Spirit? After listing the works of the flesh, followed by the fruit of the Spirit, God gives us instruction concerning our walk in the Spirit in **Galatians 5:25** *"And they that are Christ's have crucified the flesh with the affections and lusts. If we live in the Spirit, let us also walk in the Spirit."*

You must crucify your flesh daily, sometimes hourly. In eating right and exercising I've had to tell my body many times a day, "I don't care if you don't feel like exercising… you'll do what I require you to do and when I require you to do it." I don't always "feel" like getting up early to work out. I don't always "feel" like eating right. But if I want positive results tomorrow I need to make positive changes today. And that includes me disciplining my body.

So Check Your Flesh with Questions

Self-control will master your flesh and to get in control of the situation you must ask yourself some key questions that will help you learn self-control:

- "Am I pleasing God in the way I am thinking about this?"
- "What is driving me to make this decision?"
- "How will it affect me"?
- "How will it affect others"?

We cannot ignore the issue of controlling our flesh. Whatever you refuse to conquer will eventually conquer you. There is definitely a war going on and your spirit, the real you, must win.

- How long are you willing to control or not control yourself?
- What are you holding on to that is worth the loss of the prize, or goal God has set before you?

Are you ready to correct yourself in this area of self-control? Do you really think you can't deny yourself that extra helping? Is it really painful to walk away from that extra cookie? Is denying yourself that bag of chips so painful that it's in the same category as death and dismemberment in your mind?

Sometimes it is not easy to deny yourself. It's not easy to go without something you desperately want, or to give up something you dearly prize, or to lose something you cherish. But sometimes for the sake of a higher, more excellent character of life, denial is necessary. You *can* deny yourself. You *can* say no to yourself. It is not the end of all things if you have to suffer discomfort. You *can* stand it. You really can.

Romans 12:1-2 *"And so, dear brothers and sisters, I plead with you to give your bodies to God because of all He has done for you. Let them be a living and holy sacrifice – the kind He will find acceptable. This is truly the way to worship Him. Don't copy the behavior and customs of this world, but let God transform you into a new person by changing the way you think. Then you will learn to know God's will for you, which is good and pleasing and perfect."*

If you will become a living sacrifice by giving up the thoughts and attitudes that have kept you out of control, you will find freedom from bad habits, laziness, overeating, sexual sins, or anything that is controlling you!

Ultimately, you will make the choice to exercise self-control. In every situation you can have self-control by admitting you have choices and you make them. No one makes them for you. You are responsible for what you are doing. You must be prepared to accept the consequences of your behavior, whether good or bad. But self-control can become a part of your life as you diligently cultivate it, as you reject discouragement, and encourage yourself with the truth of God's Word. ***"Let us not be weary in well doing: for in due season we shall reap, if we faint not."*** **(Galatians 6:9)**

I continue to work on this fruit of self-control daily, as we all do. And as I continue to grow and develop in this character trait necessary to my Christian walk there were more lessons for me to learn on the way to the scale. The Lord was not dealing with others in my life, He was dealing with *me* – one person, and what exactly is enough for one person.

Chapter Four

THAT'S JUST NOT ENOUGH LORD

I was so excited to eat my first meal after my initial meeting with Weight Watchers. I had calculated how many points I would be allotted each day, made a menu for the week and researched how many points each food was worth for the following days eating plan. (I know, it doesn't take a lot to excite me).

My breakfast the next morning was healthy and low in points but when it came to lunch we ran through a fast food restaurant where I could have one crunchy taco for 4 points. I had two. After the tacos it wasn't too long into the afternoon that I was hungry again. So I ate an apple. When I got home I began cooking our evening meal, trying to impress my husband with a good tasting healthy meal. I weighed and measured everything and filled a large dinner plate, only to discover that the calculated amount of food was much smaller than a large dinner plate.

Most of us can recognize if we are eating healthy or not, but how many of us really pay attention to the amount of food we are taking in on a daily basis? This amount of food adds up over the weeks, months and years. It shouldn't surprise us at all when we gain a significant amount of weight, or that we haven't lost the twenty pounds we resolved to lose at the beginning of the year.

In our home we usually ate family style where you put the food on the table, fill your own plate, and continue eating until the food is gone, or your belly is full, whichever comes first. I honestly didn't think I was really eating that much food. Our daughters both left the house the same year, and as a result we had been cooking less food for a few years so I had convinced myself that I did not overeat.

But the fact is, in most American restaurants they fill your plate to the fullest, or gigantor-size at your request. I'm sure this offer of excessiveness is due to the fact that most Americans don't want to pay for their meal and afterward go away hungry. Subsequently, we have trained ourselves to eat enough food for two, and sometimes three people.

So here I was, looking at my plate that actually looked half empty and I said "This isn't enough for me". Surprised at my own words I thought, "Why is that? Am I a special case that I would deserve more food than a normal person? Am I so big that I cannot survive on a normal amount of food? What is normal? Has normal changed throughout the years? Do we exert ourselves more in the 21st Century that we need an excessive amount of food to fuel our bodies?"

Every family has stories of ancestors that have farmed fields, raised barns, mined coal, built bridges, etc., all tasks requiring much more physical work than our jobs today. And the women were not home watching television while the men were physically exerting themselves to provide for their families. The women were making the meals from the fresh food they had gardened and canned. Instead of popping a meal in the microwave, they were chopping the wood for the next meal to be cooked in the old stove, and quilting blankets for their families' warmth. They were sewing clothes and mending socks, ironing garments and cleaning the home WITHOUT vacuums, dishwashers, or trash compactors.

And yet they did all this on smaller amounts of food than what we think we deserve today. We can be sure the food portions were smaller due to the fact most families had multiple children. Even if some had only one child, everyone went through times of lack and most of us have ancestors that survived the great depression. Our bodies require much less food than we think we really need.

I survived that first meal and many more to come and to my amazement I really didn't feel hungry or deprived. Now when I ate I felt satisfied not stuffed. After learning to eat in proportion to my size the Holy Spirit said to me "You need to start reading labels".

Reading Labels

I hated reading labels. When I did my grocery shopping I was usually in a speed race to the checker. I can't really explain the rush to get through the store in record time but I can tell you I was always in a hurry. And now the Lord was requiring me to slow down and read labels.

The next day I took my new grocery list to the store, grabbed a basket, got out my WW Point Finder, and began my pursuit of low point food. My daughter had been telling me about the dangers of food high in sugar so I looked at the first five ingredients in pursuit of food low in sugar. Then I looked at the fiber grams, the fat grams and the calorie content. These last three numbers helped me figure out the points that Weight Watchers allocated to that particular food. I was ready to put the item in the basket and the Holy Spirit said "Look at the serving size". I was actually looking at one of those pre-made mashed potatoes and the serving size read, 1 serving = ½ cup. I heard the Holy Spirit say "1/2 cup is enough for one person and you are one person".

Mashed potatoes were one of my favorite foods and like I said previously, our usual custom was to put the large bowl of potatoes on the table and we would eat them till the bowl was empty or our tummy was full. More often than not, it was the former of the two. Now I was going to have to limit myself to only ½ cup? That's not enough for me!

Why was that such a problem for me? Why was my flesh so out of control in this area? Was I going to let this flesh continue to rule me? Or did I really want the help of the Holy Spirit? Lord, I not only want your help but I *need* your help. Give me grace to learn this lesson. He reminded me of what the Apostle Paul spoke about in ***Romans 6:11*** under the inspiration of the Holy Spirit. ***"Reckon yourself dead…"***. Reckon who dead?

Recon Yourself Dead

In chapter three we talked about our three part being found in **I Thessalonians 5:23**. We are Spirit, soul and body. Your spirit is the inner man, the real you, the part of you that will live forever. If you are "in Christ" through the new birth, you will immediately leave your body when your body gives up and you will be in the presence of the Lord **(II Corinthians 5:8)**. Your soul is your mind, will and emotions and it is your soul that must be renewed by the Word of God. Then the more you are in the Word the more your will and emotions will line up with the Word and you will change and become more like Jesus.

Now your body is the house that your spirit lives in. I've heard it called your "earth suit" and you have to have this earth suit to live on earth just as an astronaut must have a space suit to walk on the moon.

So what do we reckon dead? Not our body because we cannot live on earth without this body. It cannot be our spirit because God has made that alive by coming to live in our spirit. So we must reckon our soul – mind, will and emotions, dead. Every time my mind, will or emotions wants to do something that is opposed to what God wants, I need to reckon it dead.

My husband talks about reckoning ourselves dead as if we *were* dead. He says "A dead man doesn't respond". How do I not respond when my emotions want to explode? How can I die to my emotions? When did I die?

Galatians 2:20 tells us exactly when we died. *"I am crucified with Christ: nevertheless I live; yet not I, but Christ liveth in me: and the life which I now live in the flesh I live by the faith of the Son of God, who loved me, and gave himself for me."*

Did you see that? When Jesus was crucified we were crucified. Now this can get a little tricky to understand. What does God mean when He says "We are dead but yet we live"? It all depends on who you identify with and I choose to identify myself with Christ.

In Mark Hankins' book The Power of Identification with Christ he says some identify themselves with their race, religion or their old sin nature under Adam. Others identify themselves with their career and still others with problems and abuses they have encountered in life. But there is a stronger identification than what has happened to us naturally, or what we do, or what color our skin might be. IN CHRIST, there is a whole new race. (Hankins pages 12-14).

In his book <u>New Creation Realities</u> E.W. Kenyon said "Your spiritual identification is stronger than your physical identification." In Him, you're a brand new creation. **2 Corinthians 5:17** tells us ***"Therefore if any man be in Christ, he is a new creature: old things are passed away; behold, all things are become new."***

Did the Holy Spirit writing through the Apostle Paul really mean "…any man…"? Think about it, "any man". Even Paul himself, the man that the Holy Spirit moved upon to pen these words, was a persecutor of Christians. He stood there as people took off their cloaks to stone Stephen for preaching Jesus Christ. Yes, He meant "any man". You are not bad enough, lost enough, have not done enough or sinned enough that you cannot take on the nature of Jesus Christ.

In E.W.Kenyon's book <u>New Creation Realities</u> he talks about being a new creation in Christ Jesus. If you are IN CHRIST you are a "new creature". Some translations say "a new creation". The Deane translation says ***"…and a true Christian is not merely a man altered, but a man remade…"***. You're old nature has died, been destroyed and you are completely new. The old sinful nature that links you with satan has stopped being, and a new nature, God's own nature, is imparted to you. **2 Peter 1:4 "...*that you might be partakers of the divine nature...*"**

What happened to you through Jesus is greater than anything else that will ever happen to you. When we see what God has done for us in Christ, the reality of redemption will swallow up our old identity. What is the greatest miracle? The greatest miracle happens when a man receives eternal life, when a child of the devil becomes a child of God. The greatest miracle supersedes the greatest pain. (Kenyon: page 44).

What do I mean by identifying with the old sin nature or Adam? Your first birth, the day you entered this world, that birth identified you with Adam, the first Adam. One man, Adam has affected everyone who was ever born. When Adam sinned, the whole human race sinned. God tells us that in **Romans 5:17 *"Through one man's disobedience all were made sinners."***

You might think your life is your own but what you do affects a lot more than just you. When you choose to disobey God it affects your children, your children's children and their children. It also affects others around you that are watching your relationship with God. You are an ambassador for Christ – representing Him **(II Corinthians 5:20).** Keep following Jesus because others are following you.

You could say "it's not fair that one man, Adam,

could have this effect on every man. I didn't choose to be born this way". But that's the way God made it and the same law that allowed one man to affect every man is also the same law that allowed Jesus Christ, the last Adam, to take the condition the first Adam had of sin, the curse, shame, and death.

> **I Cor 15:45-49** *NLT* *"The Scriptures tell us, The first man, Adam, became a living person." But the last Adam — that is, Christ — is a life-giving Spirit. What came first was the natural body, then the spiritual body comes later. Adam, the first man, was made from the dust of the earth, while Christ, the second Man, came from heaven. Every human being has an earthly body just like Adam's, but our heavenly bodies will be just like Christ's. Just as we are now like Adam, the man of the earth, so we will someday be like Christ, the Man from heaven."*

So how are we made in the image of Christ? How do we now identify with Christ? When you are born the second time, we call it being "born again". The power of His resurrection identifies you with a whole new creation. You're not the same person anymore. You can no longer identify only with your natural family. You are now identified with Christ.

How could Jesus Christ, one man, die on the cross and His death be for every man? It's simply a law of identification. We were all identified with one man, Adam. This one man, Adam, affected every person.

So God simply took the same law that allowed one man to mess up everyone, and He allowed one man to redeem everyone.

The Laubach translation puts **Romans 5:17** this way *"That one man, Adam, when he sinned, put all men under the rule of death. But that other Man, JESUS CHRIST, makes men right with God so that they shall live and rule like kings. This He does for all who accept God's rich forgiving love and His free gift."*

If you accept God's forgiving love and His free gift of eternal life through Jesus Christ, then you accept that the other man, Jesus Christ, the "second Adam", makes you right with God and you shall live like kings, and rule like kings.

There is no hope for man's condition without Jesus. There is no hope for man outside of the blood of Jesus because **"life is in the blood" (Leviticus 17:11).** Man's condition cannot be corrected by reading a book or trying to do better. He cannot correct his behavior. He is a sinner by nature, and he cannot change himself. Only the blood of Jesus and the power of the Gospel can change a person. A person must lose his identity in Adam and get identified with Christ, the last Adam.

In Christ, you establish a whole new identity that changes you, your thinking, your direction, and everything about you. You are not in Adam; you are in Christ. You've got to get born again. He took that into Himself, died with it, and made it so that the moment you receive Jesus Christ by faith, His death becomes your death. But on the other hand, His resurrection becomes your resurrection and His righteousness – your righteousness. (Hankins pages 38-40)

Once you understand this it makes it easier to tell yourself that ½ cup of potatoes is enough for any dead man. In fact, if I am just one person then any additional food would be only what that dead man would be wanting and I don't want to feed her.

Desiring too much food was a problem that the Holy Spirit was helping me to conquer, but a new issue rose up that He would begin to help me to learn. The issue of physically moving my body more and enjoying it.

Chapter Five

LEARN TO PLAY

Most of us have read the verse in **1 Timothy 4:8** that says *"For bodily exercise profiteth little: but godliness is profitable unto all things, having promise of the life that now is, and of that which is to come."* The Amplified Bible translates this verse *"For physical training is of some value (useful for a little), but godliness (spiritual training) is useful and of value in everything and in every way, for it holds promise for the present life and also for the life which is to come."* Be assured, when this life on earth is over, there is an eternal life which is to come.

I had gotten so busy in spiritual training that I was applying this verse as if it said *"...bodily exercise profits none."* By thinking "none" instead of "little" I was getting **NO** (none, nada, zip) profit in my body from exercise because I wasn't exercising my body.

We have a hard time with the word "exercise" because we associate the expression with feelings of distress, discomfort, pain and sometimes embarrassment. Moving our bodies was never intended to make us emotionally uncomfortable. Moving our bodies (a.k.a., exercise) is simply needed to keep our bodies fit and prepared for use. Previous to the Industrial Age, most people needed to move their bodies to get their work accomplished (farming, housework, etc.). Now much of our work is accomplished while we sit at a desk and we don't have occasion to move our bodies enough to keep them healthy.

As I mentioned in the introduction of this book, one of the reasons I was so compelled to lose weight was that I was so physically unfit that I knew I would not have the stamina or endurance to help people in a disaster. I realized this condition of being physically unfit was under **my** control. With God's Grace I could improve and change my state of physical fitness.

Training ourselves in godliness is of utmost importance. However, we cannot ignore the reality that we live in a physical body. This physical body is also known as the ***"temple of God". (I Corinthians 3:16).*** It is imperative that we take care of His "temple" in order to live on this earth and accomplish God's purposes in our lives. So where do we begin re-training our bodies to move?

When we're young we tend to move continuously. I watch my grandchildren and even when they are laying down, they are not still. As babies they can be lying on their back with bottle in hand, but kicking one leg in the air. Do you think we adults could keep one leg kicking for a significant amount of time while lying on our back drinking a sports bottle of milk?

After I had lost about ten pounds I woke up one morning and as I focused my eyes I was staring at what I saw every morning for over two years. <u>**A treadmill!**</u>

We had purchased this quality treadmill back in 2001 and had used it periodically. However, most recently it had just become another piece of furniture in our bedroom. I would lay in bed looking at that thing as if I could raise my metabolism by simply gazing at the apparatus. I knew what *could* happen if I returned to a walking routine but I wasn't sure that I really wanted to commit to the time it takes. I remembered the healthy feeling of my heart beating, and the clarity of mind I had when I had used it before. Nonetheless, I remained immobile as I dreamt of what had once been.

The Lord had already been dealing with me about self-control, but I wasn't sure I was ready to obligate myself to giving up sleep to operate this contraption several times a week and if I were to add an exercise routine to my daily schedule then giving up sleep was my only option. I was already getting up about 6:30 a.m. to prepare for the day. But if I was going to include exercise in my morning schedule I would have to get up at 5:30 a.m. **There was nothing I could leave out……..**

It is necessary for me to spend time with the Lord in the morning because I concur with the prophet Jeremiah, ***"Your Words are what sustain me. They bring me great joy and are my heart's delight, for I bear Your name, O Lord God Almighty." (Jeremiah 15:16 NLT).***   I cannot take the Word of God for granted. There has been too much blood shed to get His Word to us. Not only did Jesus shed His blood for the forgiveness of our sins, but others throughout history shed their blood to get the Bible in the hands of the people so that it could be read by all men. So with the help of the Holy Spirit I intend to read it, understand it and apply it to my life. I can't start my day without Him.

It's also very important for me to have a good healthy breakfast to help jump-start my metabolism. Then there are the usual daily necessities of showering, dressing, make-up and hair, feeding the dog, straightening up the house, doing the morning dishes, putting another load in the washer and getting out the door to get to work on time. That doesn't include any phone calls that might very well come in.

So as I lay in bed the questions began as the Holy Spirit spoke to my heart. *"Are you serious about bringing glory to me through your body?" "Are you serious about fulfilling your purpose?" "Are you serious about being healthy?"* Of course I am, Lord! *"Then you need to use that treadmill for more than a fixture"*.

After responding to the Lord, I can tell you the only reason I got on that treadmill *that* morning was because I want to obey the Lord in *all* things. Isn't that the aspiration of all of us? Therefore, I must be willing **_and_** obedient (Isaiah 1:19).

Obedient to what? The Bible says in **I Corinthians 6:20** ***"For you are bought with a price: therefore glorify God in your body, and in your spirit, which are God's."*** Did Jesus shed His blood to purchase me? Definitely! So am I bringing glory to God in my body? Honestly? No. I needed to start taking care of this temple that the Holy Spirit is living in.

I quickly jumped out of bed, put on my sweats, washed my face, laced up my tennis shoes, got a glass of water, and stepped up to the treadmill for one of the biggest workouts of my year. I started out slowly and kept increasing the speed until I was at a comfortable 3 mph. Then I did everything I could to stay on that machine for a whopping five minutes. I asked myself "what happened to you?" When I had stopped my walking program a few years prior to this I was up to three miles in a half-hour! Now I couldn't even walk moderately for five minutes. How humiliating! I had stopped walking and now my body didn't want to walk. Well that called for a challenge and I'm always up for a challenge.

I challenged myself to increase my walking by at least one minute every day. Then I began to increase my speed until I had re-trained my body to walk at least 45 minutes at a fast pace. It took hardly no time at all to start feeling better. We've all read reports of research that proves walking clears your mind, causes your heart to beat effectively and even helps with depression. It would benefit everyone to walk more.

Once I got in the daily habit of walking my husband wanted to begin. We love the vigorous competition we get into over the amount of miles we walk and the speed in which we accomplish those miles. Some marriages may not enjoy the competition but in ours the pleasant rivalry sparks excitement. We quickly discovered that it was difficult to wait for the other to complete their miles, so for Christmas we made more quality additions to our exercise routine. We purchased a stationary bike and a stability ball. We also got out the dumb-bells we inherited from our daughters when they left home and now our routine consisted of a half-hour on one piece of equipment and then we would switch. Afterwards we would use the small items to cool down and/or work on trouble spots. Believe me, I had a lot of spots that were troubled!

Discipline is the Key

Now that I enjoy exercise I no longer stick to mornings alone. *Enjoy*, you say? How did I get from "having" to work out to sincerely enjoying exercise? I didn't always *feel* like working out. Some mornings I would lay in bed, not *wanting* to exercise at all. But then I (the spirit-man) would say to me (my body), **"I don't care what you (body) feel like doing, I'm (spirit) in control and you (body) will do what I (spirit) tell you (body) to do!"** Of course I didn't speak in parenthesis to myself. I'm just doing what the Apostle Paul did when he said *"I discipline my body like an athlete, training it to do what it should." (I Corinthians 9:27 NLT).*

What exactly does it mean to *discipline* your body? Merriam-Webster On-line Dictionary says one form of discipline is "control gained by enforcing obedience or order." I want to gain control over my body. So I must enforce it to obey or do what I (spirit-man) order it to do. My body is in training and my spirit-man will be in control.

You can train your body to do anything you want it to do, but why would you? In my case it was necessary to train my body so I would be in good shape physically to help others in need. According to the Merriam-Webster On-line Dictionary, to train means "to form by instruction, discipline, or drill; to teach so as to make fit, qualified, or proficient; to make prepared (as by exercise) for a test of skill." Do you remember what Paul said in **I Corinthians 9:27?** The Amplified Bible reads: ***"But [like a boxer] I buffet my body [handle it roughly, discipline it by hardships] and subdue it, for fear that after proclaiming to others the Gospel and things pertaining to it, I myself should become unfit [not stand the test, be unapproved and rejected as a counterfeit]."*** I certainly do not want to be unfit or disqualified. There is much to do in the Kingdom of God and this Army of the Lord will be well trained.

Exercise was Meant to be Fun

It is important to note that exercise does not have to be boring and monotonous. Young people are exercising all the time and don't even know it. When did we accept the lie that exercise is not fun?

As a teenager I loved to play tennis. I don't know if one would consider me any good or not, but I loved the game. For the most part, I was raised in the desert region of Southern California and most schools, including mine, taught tennis as part of the Physical Education program. (By the way, I think it's a shame that schools no longer place value or encourage living an active lifestyle by insisting on mandatory physical education classes.) When I met my husband, something we had in common was that he too played tennis in school and was rather good at it. For some reason we didn't play together while we were courting, nor for the first ten years of our marriage. We always had good intentions but good intentions didn't get us on the court. And then my husband surprised me on our tenth anniversary by replacing our old tennis racquets and taking me to play on the local courts.

Even though it had been a decade since I played a match, the rules of the game came back quickly. I couldn't move very fast due to the extra pounds I had put on, but I realized I still loved the game. However, that love for the game didn't get me moving but it did give me an idea for my daughters. "Let's get them on the courts." I guess you could say we lived vicariously through them as they learned the game.

We enrolled them in tennis lessons with a small group of children and one tennis instructor. One by one the other children gave up on the weekly tennis lessons but we kept our girls playing. The instructor was very impressed that our elementary girls could take the heat so well, but with the promise of a Dairy Queen cone at the end of each lesson our girls were more than willing to accommodate. At times my husband would play a match with them but I didn't feel like I could keep up with their speed. So I didn't even try…until I was on the road to losing weight in 2006.

One Wednesday night at church I heard one of the young women in our church saying she'd like to play tennis but no one will play with her. All of the sudden these words came out of my mouth, "I'll play". Inside I thought, "What do you mean you'll play?

You haven't played in years". But I didn't want to disappoint her so I kept my thoughts to myself.

I went home and refreshed my mind on the rules of the game by going to the worldwide web. Then my husband and I both showed up for a game on the high school courts and sure enough she was on time. The first ball was served, returned and served again. Before we knew it we had played an hour of tennis and without realizing it we were enjoying ourselves. My husband was still good at the game and no one could beat him.

A few days later we played our daughter and son-in-law, and rescheduled our games for every week with our original team. What a wonderful way to exercise when you re-learn something you love.

Every chance I get I play tennis with someone. I went to visit my family in central California and asked my nephew if he had some tennis racquets. He did, and after my father lovingly drove us around to find tennis balls late one night, we found a court the next morning where my mom, my nephew and I could all play. We laughed, played and burned calories all at the same time. It really is a joy to play with your family. Not only do you get the much needed exercise but you learn about your family and really enjoy their company.

No matter where I am in the country, I have found that I can play tennis. My youngest daughter was expected to deliver her first child and lived in a condo in the desert of southern California. I went to stay with her and her husband for a month to help with their new addition and they had tennis courts at their complex. My son-in-law had not really played tennis before, so we started slowly. Within a few matches we discovered he was a natural at the game. His father began to join the tennis team we had created and he too rediscovered his love and great ability for the game. What fun we have when we re-learn to "play". And there are so many different ways to "play".

Another way to "play" is to ride bikes. Most children ride bikes all the time as their source of limited transportation, and for most of us it was a step of independence when we received our first bike. After the crashes, bumps and bruises you get from trial and error, you start to love the freedom you feel as the wind blows through your hair as you ride through the neighborhood. The older I got the farther I was allowed to ride until one day I had the whole town I could cycle through if I so chose.

In 2006 my husband and I had gone to the east coast for the first time in our lives to attend a convention and also visit with some very dear friends. Our friends live on the coast of New Jersey. The beauty of the ocean, the trees, and the quaint little villages along the shore enhanced what we remember as one of our best vacations ever. The week we were in New Jersey our friends' daughter, a recent college graduate, was training for the "Tour de Tucson". She was preparing to ride one morning and asked if I wanted to go. Again, without even thinking about it, I said "sure". I was fine until they brought this pricey bike around the building for me to ride. I began to wonder how I would pay for this thing if I were to wreck. However I got on and circled the cul-de-sac a few times. It's true! You never forget how to ride a bike.

We hoisted this 7lb bike onto the bike rack and we headed for the riding trail. She and I cycled all through the beautiful woods of New Jersey and viewed the lakes and landscape that you'll only see in that region of the United States. When we were done we had cycled about nine miles. Now that isn't a century of 106 miles but for me, that was a huge accomplishment. I returned home and asked the Lord for a bike. Guess what He gave me? That's right, a bike. In fact, because Bullhead City is so rocky I needed a mountain bike with the wider tires and that's exactly what the Lord gave me. My husband replaced the tires, bought me a bike helmet and I was on my way.

A year later I went to visit family in Washington and my niece took me for a beautiful ride in their neighborhood. I enjoyed it and the Lord blessed me with a better bike and blessed my husband as well. At the writing of this book I ride on a regular basis ten or more miles a day. I have found that I really enjoy the ride.

There was something else I tried, just for fun. While staying in the desert with my daughter, my son-in-law brought home a motorcycle he was interested in purchasing. He showed it to me and said "You want to ride?" My answer was quicker than my thoughts again and I said "You bet I do". I had Lindsay take a picture of me in case I didn't return the same way I left. Then down the streets of Palm Desert we went. Would I have gotten on that bike six months prior to the weight loss? Definitely not. But I was finding new things I could do and I was having fun doing them. **Exercise has proven to be liberating not laborious.**

Does this take more time? In fact, it does. But what we've done is replaced time we spent watching television with some sort of exercise. Sometimes we'll go to the gym, and other times we'll take a walk around our neighborhood, or get on the bike, or get to the tennis courts. Our next goal is to learn about hiking and go hiking in our local mountain range. These things can even be more fun when done with other people. Try it! You may re-learn the joy of "playing".

Now that I had the importance of exercise down, the Lord was requiring of me accountability to more than one.

Chapter Six

THE NEED TO KNOW

Proverbs 2:11 in the Amplified Bible says *"Discretion shall watch over you, understanding shall keep you."* Over the years I've endeavored to learn discretion, albeit through trial and error.

What exactly is discretion? According to the dictionary discretion is being careful about what one says or does or the ability to keep silent. The dictionary also says that this quality is regulated by one's own choice. For instance, when you want to lose weight it is "left up to one's discretion," how you do that. That means it is left up to a person's choice. You cannot decide what another person's discretion is, for it has to do with his own conclusion to the question, *How do I think I should do this?* You are a person of discretion because you choose to be a person of discretion. However, discretion isn't an attribute that you either possess or don't. Rather, it is a quality that lives in various measure inside every person.

The Lord teaches us that discretion watches over us. The King James Version says it will preserve us. The original Hebrew word is *shamar* which means to watch and guard us as a watchman would watch over his post. Discretion will do that for you. Another words, it is very important to choose to be careful about what we say and do. There are some things that not everyone needs to know about and I felt my struggles with weight were one of those areas.

It was obvious that I was overweight by quite a few pounds, but I really didn't want to share with people the emanate issues I had with low self-esteem and lack of confidence due to the weight. Although discretion is an important part of our character development and is still required at times, there was something else God was asking of me and that was accountability.

The word accountability comes from the Greek word *logizomai* which means to keep a record of; to reckon or account and treat accordingly; to weigh the reasons, deliberate and meditate.

When you are accountable to another person you open yourself up to having them keep record of your accomplishments and perhaps help you with the reasons for weight-loss or no weight-loss. Why is this so difficult? Is it because when it comes down to the bottom line we want to do what we want to do and we don't want anyone to tell us any different? Is that pride? Is that rebellion?

It would be a lot easier to not be rebellious if we didn't have to answer to anyone. I think a lot of my problem for so many years was that no one was going to tell me what to eat. I could figure this out on my own. And so I did. And as I did I got larger and larger. All because I didn't want anyone telling me what to do.

Once I opened myself to accountability I was going to have to trust that God had people to speak into my life and help me keep record of my successes and failures. This is part of his plan for His family. To help one another with our struggles. Can we really be vulnerable to each other without being offended? I believe we can.

Being Accountable to a Stranger

When the Lord was dealing with me to join Weight Watchers, I was reluctant to attend because I would have to get on a scale in front of a stranger every week. I was under the impression that if I stayed on program all week I would lose weight and this would make my leader and me happy. I also thought that if I veered from the program the scale would reveal my "sin" of overeating, my leader would "lecture" me on how I had failed, and I would end up crying. But glory to God, this never happened.

I did my best to stay on program and sometimes I lost big and sometimes I lost little. There were times I gained and many times that my weight didn't go up or down on the scale, even though I had a so-called "perfect week." I began to realize that the scale would not always show proof of my efforts to lose the weight I was expecting to have lost. It is true, the more I was consistent with staying on program the more consistently I lost weight but letting another person help me keep record of my successes and failures helped me remain accountable.

Being Accountable to Friends

Hey God, I don't like this. Just who are you going to require me to be accountable to? I have many in my circle of friends, those that influence me and those I influence. There are also many diverse facets of my life. I have family, church-family, friends, co-workers, pastor-friends, and acquaintances. My hope was that God would require me to be account-able to only one but the fact was as I began to lose a significant amount of weight people began noticing and then they began to watch what I was eating and how active I had become. In fact they all had their own opinion of what works and what doesn't work. Discussion of my weight loss had come to the fore-front and accountability had gone from one person to a few and now to many.

Was God requiring me to be accountable to everyone? Would I have to be open and vulnerable with everyone I know and be willing to share in my attempt to lose weight? Why couldn't I exercise discretion in *this* area of my life? Why did I feel like I was in a "fish-bowl"? Because God was also speaking to many of them to get in control of their eating and He was using my successes to encourage them.

Accountable to Family

As I mentioned in chapter two, telling my friends that I was working on my weight resulted in their assistance not resistance. I wasn't so sure it would be that easy with family because receiving support from family and friends was of utmost importance to my success.

I am so thankful for family that is encouraging. I had lost 64 lbs by the time I went to visit my parents in the spring of 2006. When I arrived at their home my mom said she didn't want to sabotage everything I had done so she asked me what I could eat. We discussed different types of healthy foods that I had been eating and took off to the store. We brought back fresh vegetables, fresh fruit, whole grains, chicken and little 100 Calorie packs of goodies in case we had a sweet tooth attack. My mother and I went for walks in the morning and we played tennis with my nephews. When I returned home the following Monday I had still lost 2.6 pounds. Thanks to family you can enjoy their company and still eat healthy. After all, there are other things to do with family besides eat.

We took another trip that year to visit my mother-in-law and preach in Arkansas. While we were in the mid-west we stayed with my husband's family in Arkansas and Oklahoma and they were just as helpful in my attempt to lose weight even though the food choices were very "southern".

I must share with you what kind of food our loved ones eat on a regular basis. First of all, most things are fried, even vegetables. There are some vegetables cooked in water and not fried, but sugar has been diluted into the water. You "must" have biscuits with every meal. These discs of culinary delight are hot, soft, flaky, buttery, homemade and extremely tantalizing. At breakfast extra goodness (and calories) are added by drenching the mouth-watering biscuits in good ole' country sausage gravy.

With all the good country cooks around I was surprised that every person was supportive of my efforts to lose weight. They continued to cook their "regular" food but added a fresh salad and fresh fruit. I just limited my portions on the other.

My mother-in-law loved biscuits and gravy for breakfast. One morning we woke up and all the electricity was out in her little mid-western Oklahoman town. We decided to go out for breakfast and she said "I want to take you to the best biscuits and gravy in town." I wasn't intending on ordering biscuits and gravy but I went along for the fun. We started down the road and she pointed to a little gas station store. My husband asked "Here?" She nodded "Yes." Tim asked one more time to be sure; "They have the best biscuits and gravy in town?" So, we walked in and discovered that their electricity was out along with the rest of the town. I began to scour the aisles of the little store to find something we could fuel our bodies with. Mom, who was a professional cook before retiring, walked into the little restaurant off to the side of the store and said "We'd like some biscuits and gravy". The clerk answered "There's no electricity". Mom went behind the stove, noticed it was powered by gas and explained how they could heat everything we wanted on the grill. We took our place at the only booth in the restaurant and ate biscuits, gravy and bacon. Those were the only things they cooked for us, so I ate them. When I returned to the house I looked up the point value of the foods I had consumed and calculated that I had eaten the whole day's worth of points in one sitting. However, I had extra points allotted to me for "emergencies" just like this. I just wasn't sure if this constituted an "emergency" or not.

We ate as healthy as we could but when I returned to the scale I hadn't lost any weight. However, I also didn't gain any weight. Letting family know what you are working on will actually enhance your weight loss efforts, not be detrimental. Unless, you have a family constantly trying to get you off-course. Unfortunately, there are families like that.

I've seen some families that don't seem to appreciate the efforts of those trying to get healthy. In fact, they encourage that person to eat out of control by saying things like "Come on, you've lost enough weight", "You're looking a little too thin for this family", "What makes you think you can lose that much weight?", "We worked so hard to fry up this chicken and gravy", "I bought this pie especially for you", "We're going out of town and you know how we love to eat at 'x'!"

What do you say to family and friends that say they love you with food. First of all, you remind yourself of your goals. Why is it that you're losing weight in the first place? For me, it was to get physically fit, to receive healing in my body, and to be fit to do what God had called me to do. When you know the reasons you are getting healthy then no one can deter you from that goal, if you will not let them.

Secondly, you tell your family that you don't love them any less if you don't eat the food they've prepared or purchased especially for you. In fact, you may have to resign from eating with them for awhile if it really bothers them that you are making healthy choices.

I'm not sure what the reasons are that some will try to disrupt your weight loss efforts. It may be because they're jealous that you are doing what they've dreamt of doing for so long. I'm not sure if it's because they don't want you to be able to do things that they can't. You know kind of like the ole' saying "misery loves company". But if your reasons are to live long so you can see your children's children and perhaps their children, then you need to plant your feet in the ground of good health and refuse to be moved. If your reasons are just so you have the ability to move your body at your particular age, then stay on track.

If you eat what your family or friends are encouraging you to eat, and the amount that they want you to eat, are they also going to be there when you can't get out of bed due to obesity? Are they going to be there when your heart can't support your weight? Are they going to be there when you're so discouraged because of your lack of self-control? Or have you turned your self-control over to their control?

Being accountable to family was one thing but I had also become accountable to my leader. During my weight-loss journey I noticed that I was very _aware_ of the days of the week and how many days I had till weigh-in. I didn't really understand at first because everything my leader was lecturing us on was merely common sense. Or perhaps the sense I had was not so common. Being accountable to her simply meant that I was going to show up every week and get on that scale no matter what. It was one of the hardest things I did to get on that scale when I didn't think I had had a very successful week. But I had to be honest with myself. Just because I didn't get on the scale didn't mean I didn't mess up. It just meant I didn't want to know the truth. But the fact was, I was at a place in my life that I *did* want to know the truth, no matter what it was. And I would live with that and make the appropriate changes.

When it comes to spiritual things we learn to be **"doers of the Word of God and not hearers only"** but now I had to apply that same principle to losing weight. I would hear the lesson, even take notes on some mantras of hers, and then go home and do what I heard. Concerning spiritual things the Apostle Paul said in **Hebrews 2:1** *"Therefore we ought to give the more earnest heed to the things which we <u>have</u> heard, lest at any time we should let them slip."* Notice it's the things which we *have* heard that we mustn't let slip. In the natural, we've all heard what it takes to eat right, exercise and control ourselves but if we don't pay attention to it by doing it, these things will slip away and we won't see any changes.

I know for some people you may not want to answer to your spouse, but for me, my husband was another person I had made myself accountable to. I would let him know very specific goals and ask for his help in achieving them. For instance, I want to lose "x" amount of pounds before we go to such-and-such place. Or, I want to be a size "x" before a certain event. Another goal I learned to use was "I want to <u>*'do'*</u> such-and-such when I reach a certain weight". While losing weight I reached one goal and then I would celebrate that accomplishment and immediately set another goal. In order to help with your ultimate objective its better if the celebration is not edible.

As the days of the week passed I not only thought of the lesson we had learned, but I found myself anticipating the lesson to be taught the next week. The more I learned and the closer I got to goal the less it bothered me that everyone knew I was losing weight. Praise the Lord, I arrived at the place emotionally that it didn't bother me what people thought anymore because I was not doing this for them.   I knew what I had to do to lose weight and no one was going to say anything or force me to eat anything I didn't want to eat. I had gained weight because of a lack of accountability and now I was losing weight because of a multiplicity of accountability.

However, now the Holy Spirit was taking me to a place where I would be accountable to only Him. After all, according to **John 14:16** in the Amplified Bible, "*...the Holy Spirit is my Counselor, Helper, Intercessor, Advocate, Strengthener, and Standby...*" I first had to learn to be accountable to people, now I would be accountable to God.

Being Accountable to the Holy Spirit

The Holy Spirit is the most important teacher that we will ever have and if you've been born again, He has taken residence in you. Do we feel that same impression of accountability to Him who knows and sees all that we do? Should He not keep record of this prodigious journey? I believe He should. And He can only do that if we fellowship with Him.

The Holy Spirit knows us really well but we must fellowship with Him to know Him better. How do we do that? We talk to Him. We ask Him His opinion and for His direction. We read His love letters to us found in the Bible.

If I were a new bride and my husband were off at war, most likely he would write me everyday and share with me his innermost thoughts and feelings, his desires, his love for me and his plan for our future. What would happen if at his return he were to say "Honey, did you read my letters to you?" and I were to say "No, I didn't think it was that important". It's the same principle with reading God's Word, the Bible. God has written his love letter to us sharing who He is, what He's done for us and His plan for our future. If we want to know what that plan is, we must read His love letter to us.

The way to be accountable to God is through prayer, two-way communication. Talk to Him. Share with Him your struggles and your victories and then listen to Him for His help. God will take things in the spirit realm and move things in your natural realm, just because you asked Him to.

You may be saying right now "I don't have time to pray". That's because the devil will fight your prayer life more than any other area because he suffers the most when you pray. You must make time to pray. However, don't put your confidence in the "act of prayer" but in the God who answers prayer.

Too many times people have thought that the "act of prayer" is what changes things. But if that were the case then we should lock ourselves away for months at a time and "pray" like someone who doesn't release his faith. Don't magnify what *you* do but magnify what *God* does. You pray but God answers. It's not prayer itself that changes things. It's God who changes things and believing that He hears AND answers our prayers. **1 John 5:14-15** ***"And this is the confidence that we have in Him, that, if we ask anything according to His will, He hears us: And if we know that He hears us, whatsoever we ask, we know that we have the petitions that we desired of Him."***

Did you notice that our confidence is in that He hears us? Yes! God hears us. Prayer is more than simply speaking words into empty air. God hears us and He hears us all the time. You can be praying while you're driving, washing the dishes, vacuuming the floor and in some cases working. You don't have to wait till it's time to go to bed to "say your prayers" as you kneel beside the mattress. No, emphatically no! Jesus provided a way that you can, and should, communicate with your heavenly Father all the time, and every day.

I will say there are times for focused prayer when the Holy Spirit is directing you to spend time praying about a particular thing or listening to Him. One day I was walking around and praying in the Spirit, alone at our church, and found some trash that needed to be picked up, some flowers that needed to be straightened, really nothing that couldn't wait, and the Holy Spirit said to me "You multi-task Me". He was trying to get my attention to tell me some things but I was so busy "doing" that I wasn't settling my mind to hear from Him. So there are times to "be still" before the Lord and listen to Him.

You may be asking right now, so if I must be accountable to the Lord, if prayer is so important how do I do it? How do I know the will of God and what to pray? How does He speak to me? How do I hear Him? What does He sound like? Prayer is vitally important to your whole life, not just weight control. Shouldn't we know how to pray?

How to Pray

To Whom do we pray? The New Living Translation makes it simple in **John 16:23-24**

"At that time you won't need to ask me for anything. The truth is, you can go directly to the Father and ask Him, and He will grant your request because you use My name. You haven't done this before. Ask, using My name, and you will receive, and you will have abundant joy."

So according to the Scriptures, we pray to the Father in Jesus' name.

As I mentioned before, ***"we have confidence that He hears us when we pray according to His will" (I John 5:14-15).*** So what is God's will? God's will is already revealed in His Word, the Bible. God's Word and God's will are synonymous. If you are praying about something that is in line with God's Word, you can be confident you are praying according to God's will.

It's also important to mention here that *faith begins where the will of God is known.* God's will is revealed in His Word. In a nutshell, faith is simply taking God at His Word. Faith is believing and acting like what God has said in His Word is true! Faith is trusting God. I've heard too many people say "I don't have as much faith as Oral Roberts, or so-and-so." What you're telling me is you don't trust God as much as Oral Roberts, or so-and-so. Well we can change that because your faith can grow as you hear the Word of God because ***"faith comes by hearing the Word of God" (Romans 10:17).***

God hears your prayer the first time you pray. However, we have an enemy, satan, and he will do whatever he can to hinder us from receiving the answers to our prayers. It is at this point that we have to exercise our faith with patience. We have to maintain our belief in the promises of God. We must walk by faith and not by sight and as we stay in faith, refusing to doubt, the answer God sent to us will be manifested. Notice what God said in **Hebrews 6:12** *"That ye be not slothful, but followers of them who through faith and patience inherit the promises."* So you need both, faith *and* patience.

Another vital area to successful prayer is to say what God has said. Too many times I've seen people get up from prayer, after hearing from God, and say the opposite of what God has just told them. This negates their faith. They are now speaking and hearing the opposite of what they just asked of God. How can you believe one thing and speak another? If we want to unlock the door to answered prayer we must verbally agree with what God said. **Mark 11:22-24** is one of the Scriptures that teach us this principle. *"So Jesus answered and said to them, "Have faith in God. For assuredly, I say to you, whoever SAYS to this mountain, 'Be removed and be cast into the sea,' and does not doubt in his heart, but believes that those things he SAYS will be done, he will have whatever he SAYS. Therefore I say to you, whatever things you ask when you pray, believe that you receive them, and you will have them."* Notice three times Jesus mentioned our "saying". We must learn to say what God says if we want our prayers answered.

Why is this so important to me controlling my weight? While I was losing weight I noticed something. People would say to me "You're looking so good, isn't it hard to lose weight?" And the first few times I agreed. "Oh, it's so hard". Then I realized what I was saying. "It's so hard". Well, the fact was it really wasn't that hard but I was making it harder by saying it was hard. I went to prayer and asked the Lord for His help and when I began to say "It's not hard to lose weight, in fact, the Holy Spirit is my helper and it is within my reach", I noticed it got easier. I began to believe what I was saying and so I said what I believed.

The same thing happened with exercise. I didn't always "feel" like exercising but I knew the benefits of exercising. After catching myself saying "I hate exercising" I decided to change that. I went to prayer about it and asked the Lord to help me change my attitude. I changed my words to agree with what God said. ***"I discipline my body like an athlete, training it to do what it should and I love exercising" (I Corinthians 9:27 NLT).*** I can honestly say I really do love exercising.

Go ahead, catch your words. If you're planting unfruitful words, dig them up and plant some fruitful ones. You want to reap a good harvest don't you?

Proverbs 18:21 *"Death and life are in the power of the tongue: and they that love it shall eat the fruit thereof."*

How God Talks to Me

Being accountable to God means that He will

speak to you concerning your weight control. But how exactly does He speak to us?

The number one way God speaks to us is through His Word, the Bible. As I mentioned before it is His personal love letter to us and it is *"alive and full of power [making it active, operative, energizing, and effective]; it is sharper than any two-edged sword, penetrating to the dividing line of the breath of life (soul) and [the immortal] spirit, and of joints and marrow [of the deepest parts of our nature], exposing and sifting and analyzing and judging the very thoughts and purposes of the heart."* **(Hebrews 4:12** *AMP)*.

As you open the Scriptures God will speak to you and even sift your thoughts and your hearts motives. He may reveal some things that you're not comfortable changing but if you really want to grow spiritually, yield to His correction.

Another way He speaks to us is by His Spirit. But it's important to note that His Word and Spirit will always agree. He will not tell you something that does not line up with Scripture. The Bible says in **Romans 8:14** *"For as many as are led by the Spirit of God, they are the sons of God"*. If you have accepted Jesus as your Lord and Savior according to **Romans 10:9-10**, you have been born of God and you are a son (or daughter) of God. And if you are a son (or daughter) of God you can be led by the Spirit of God.

There is an additional experience to being born again that gives us an advantage to being led by the Spirit. In one of the travels to Ephesus the Apostle Paul asked them *"Have you received the Holy Ghost since you believed? And they said unto him, we have not so much as heard whether there be any Holy Ghost….and when Paul had laid his hands upon them, the Holy Ghost came on them; and they spake with tongues, and prophesied". (Acts 19:2,6).*

When you are filled with the baptism of the Holy Spirit you have a divine connection to God. How do we know that? **1 Corinthians 14:2** *says "For he that speaketh in an unknown tongue speaketh not unto men , but unto God."* Not only can we speak to God by praying in the Spirit but also He speaks to us when we pray in the Spirit.

Notice **1 Corinthians 2:9-10** *"But as it is written, eye hath not seen, nor ear heard, neither have entered into the heart of man, the things which God hath prepared for them that love him. But God hath revealed them unto us by his Spirit: for the Spirit searcheth all things, yea, the deep things of God."* How does God reveal these great things that He has prepared for us? By His Spirit.

Another thing that happens as you pray in the Spirit (or pray in tongues) is found in **Romans 8:26-27** *"Likewise the Spirit also helpeth our infirmities: for we know not what we should pray for as we* *ought: but the Spirit Himself maketh intercession for us with groanings which cannot be uttered. And He that searcheth the hearts knoweth what is the mind of the Spirit, because He maketh intercession for the saints according to the will of God."* When you pray in the Spirit, the Holy Spirit takes over and prays according to the will of God. Who better to pray the perfect will of God than the Holy Spirit?

Although I cannot cover everything about the wonderful gift called the baptism in the Holy Spirit I found it necessary to include what I've said about Him because without praying in the Spirit I would not have succeeded in my goals of weight loss or anything else I've accomplished for the Lord. As I pray in the Spirit I find my spirit-man being edified, charged and built up. There is no better person to be accountable to than to the Holy Spirit who knows me, loves me and knows how to help me.

But don't misunderstand. The Holy Spirit will help us but He won't do it for us. I mentioned in a previous chapter that one of the fruit of the Spirit is self-control not God-control. He'll never *make* you do anything, but He will *help* you. And in helping you it will take patience on your part. There are instant miracles that God does in the lives of people. However, there are also progressive miracles. Losing weight and gaining control over your eating patterns will take time and time takes patience which led me to another lesson I learned on the way to the scale.

Chapter Seven

I DON'T HAVE TIME TO WAIT

So many times we start on a "diet" because we have somewhere to go on a specific date and 'if I could just lose 100 pounds in 2 months I'd be happy'. I know that's exaggerated but it seems we're always in a hurry when it comes to losing weight. Did you ever think that there may be a special event to attend in 2 years and if you start now you could be thin and healthy by then?

Do you ever get impatient with yourself when you're going through a process and then get irritated because you didn't reach your goal in an unrealistic amount of time? In many cases we negate what we've learned with our negative attitude of irritation. Like most people I have been working on the fruit of patience for most of my life and this was an important lesson for me on the way to the scale. In fact, I even had to exercise patience in the writing of this book. After the Lord asked me to write this

I made a schedule for myself and intended to have the book written, edited and published within four months. Needless to say that didn't happen.

In a world of microwaves, computers, the world wide web, cell phones, IPods, Iphones and PDA's we expect things to be done in the time it takes to speak or type our plans. But we don't consider the people and the process involved to accomplish those plans.

Most of us expect immediate results but the fact is we know it's impossible under most circumstances. I never expected to have a baby in a day, nor did I expect that child to grow up in a day. In fact, the only area in which we expect immediate results seems to be in the area of weight-loss. And yet we know that's impossible. Even those that opt for surgery to lose weight must comprehend that the weight will not be gone the day after surgery. And yet I found myself planning *when* I would be at my weight goal and it usually wasn't too far from when I began the journey.

Patience is a wonderful quality usually employed under difficult circumstances. But let's look at patience realistically. If you got *everything* you wanted *when* you wanted it, patience would be unnecessary because you wouldn't have to *wait* for anything. Even if you are a sweet little thing that deserves to have it right now, most things in life take time. And most things in life *are* worth waiting for.

The Fruit of the Spirit

There is a list of the fruit of the Spirit in **Galatians 5:22-24**. These are His fruit and where He goes they go. If you are born again, the Holy Spirit lives in you and so do His fruit. ***"The fruit of the Spirit is love, joy, peace, patience, kindness, goodness, faithfulness, gentleness and self-control. Against such things there is no law."*** If these are all in me then why don't I always walk in love, have joy, be patient and kind and faithful, etc., etc., etc.?

Let's look at it this way. When my grandchildren were born they were perfect, just like yours. They were beautiful little baby girls with everything God created them with. They had as many fingers and toes that I have as well as the same muscles and organs. Well, if they have the same muscles that I have they ought to be able to get up and walk and jump and run just like I can, right? Wrong! Why? Because their muscles need to be developed and to develop them they will need to use them.

The same is true with the fruit of the Spirit. If you want to walk in love you'll need to use the fruit of love on a consistent basis, and the great thing is – you'll have many opportunities to walk in love. And if you want to be patient you will need to exercise patience every chance you get in order to develop in patience. Well, in order to develop in the fruit of the Spirit we must have an understanding of what God was talking about and that takes a little bit of research. So let's look at what patience means?

The Bible says in **James 1:2-4** *says "My brethren, count it all joy when you fall into divers temptations; knowing this, that the trying of your faith worketh patience. But let patience have her perfect work, that you may be perfect and entire, wanting nothing."*

> According to Rick Renner is his book <u>Sparkling Gems of the Greek</u> the word patience is the Greek word "hupomeno" – a compound of the words "hupo" and "meno". The word "hupo" means "under, as to be underneath something". The word "meno" means "to stay or to abide". You could say that the word "meno" means "to remain in one's spot; to keep a position; to resolve to maintain some territory that has been gained". It is the state of mind that says, "This is my spot, and I'm not moving!" This word "hupomeno" is most clear when it was used in a military sense to picture soldiers who were ordered to maintain their positions even in the face of fierce combat. Their order was to stand their ground and defend what had been gained. To keep that ground, they had to be courageous to do whatever was required – no matter how hard or difficult the assignment. (Renner; 146-147).

Plateau or Patience?

I know a true plateau is when you aren't losing anything for a significant amount of time. However, I think I had lost about 60 pounds when I had come to somewhat of a plateau. I was eating so much less than what I was used to and exercising 5 to 7 times a week. Week after week I would keep this routine and happily go off to the scale only to see that I lost ¼ of a pound – sometimes ½ pound, and sometimes nothing. I told my leader it didn't make sense. My way of eating and exercising had extremely changed so I should see some extreme results. She kept saying "give it time". Sure enough one Monday night came and I got on the scale as usual only to find that I had lost 6 pounds in one week. What if I had given up on one of those weeks that I had lost nothing? What if I had said "well this doesn't work"?

One particular week that I lost ¼ of a pound I went home after the meeting to tell my husband 'if I can't lose anymore than this I'm quitting.' He quickly reminded me of the overall total I had lost and encouraged me to be patient. I responded with "Patient? Do you really know what it takes to lose 90 pounds?" "I sure don't". He calmly answered "patience". And he was right. If I were to exercise patience I would stand my ground and defend what I had gained (in my case, lost). I would keep that ground, I had to be courageous to do whatever was required – no matter how hard or difficult my assignment. And this kind of Bible-patience paid off in the end.

This kind of patience must be applied to absolutely every area of our lives. You must believe that you will succeed but you also must be patient in the process. We hear so much about faith and believing that sometimes we think if the answer to our prayer hasn't manifested within a matter of days then there isn't much to this "faith stuff". However, there is a power-twin to faith and that is **patience**. The Holy Spirit tells us in **Hebrews 6:12** *"That ye be not slothful, but followers of them who through FAITH AND PATIENCE inherit the promises."*

Faith and Patience

It is necessary for us to *believe* that we can achieve our goals with the grace of God but it is just as important to employ patience in the process. **Hebrews 10:36** *says "For you have need of patience, that, after you have done the will of God, you might receive the promise."* The New Living Translation says it like this *"Do not throw away this confident trust in the Lord, no matter what happens. Remember the great reward it brings you! Patient endurance is what you need now, so you will continue to do God's will. Then you will receive all that he has promised."* A person of Bible-patience says "I don't care how long it takes; I refuse to move from my position because I know that it is where

90

I'm supposed to be!" It's not a question *if* you will lose weight – it's only a question of *when* you will lose weight. But for you to reach that long-awaited weight goal, it is essential that you practice patience in your life.

Believe me, when I say I know what you're going through, **I really know what you're going through**. Some weeks I knew I had eaten too much of the wrong foods and I didn't know what I was going to lose when I got on that scale. In fact, I was tempted to skip the meeting but I knew the Lord had asked me to attend consistently. I would tell my husband as I left the house "I don't think I've lost anything, but I'll go anyway." And then to my surprise I would be down some. When I got home my husband would tell me that he had prayed for me. Now you understand that I didn't lose the weight at the last minute because he prayed for me. But God is merciful. Just knowing that my husband was praying for me was the support I needed to remain patient in my trial.

Watch Out for Slothfulness

Let's take another look at **Hebrews 6:12** *that says "That ye be not slothful, but followers of them who through faith and patience inherit the promises."* Why would Paul tell us not to be slothful? What does *slothful* mean?

Many times we associate slothfulness with laziness but one has nothing to do with the other. In studying patience I found that if I didn't put slothfulness away from me I would return to my old ways of eating and gain back everything I had lost.

Again, quoting Rick Renner's book <u>Sparkling Gems from the Greek</u> "Slothful" comes from the Greek word "nothros" and describes something that is dull, monotonous, or unexciting, something that is slow and sluggish; or something that has lost its speed or momentum. This "something" is still moving, but it isn't moving with the same velocity and aggressiveness it once had. It has lost the drive, thrust, impetus, pace, and speed it once possessed. This word therefore presents the idea of someone who was once zealous about something but whose zeal has now dissipated, replaced instead by neutrality. (Renner; 133).

In my past experiences of losing weight this is what would happen. I would be gun-ho at the beginning and get everything I could get to teach me to lose weight. I'd always start off good and then the excitement would wane, I would still be moving forward a little bit but not with the same enthusiasm I had when I started. My pace would slow down and I would eventually give up for lack of interest. What I needed to do was get out of my state of neutrality and run my race with fervor.

This slothfulness can come on anyone making healthy changes. If we don't change our menu or exercise program periodically it can get monotonous. In fact, there were days where I got frustrated because I couldn't figure out something different to eat for lunch. I had done away with fast food because it cost me too many points for too little food. But if I ate the same thing everyday, that got boring. So I started asking the Lord for His help. I needed fresh ideas for low-point foods. You can find some on-line but my best resource was friends that were making healthy changes as well.

Speak the Word

Still having trouble with patience? Why not begin to say what God says about you? Take a look at these Scriptures about patience:

Col 1:11 *(AMP) [We pray] that you may be invigorated and strengthened with all power according to the might of His glory, [to exercise] every kind of endurance and <u>patience</u> (perseverance and forbearance) with joy.*

Heb 10:36 *(AMP) "For you have need of steadfast <u>patience</u> and endurance, so that you may perform and fully accomplish the will of God, and thus receive and carry away [and enjoy to the full] what is promised."*

Heb 12:1-2 *(AMP) "THEREFORE THEN, since we are surrounded by so great a cloud of witnesses [who have borne testimony to the Truth], let us strip off and throw aside every encumbrance (unnecessary weight) and* *that sin which so readily (deftly and cleverly) clings to and entangles us, and let us run with* <u>*patient endurance*</u> *and steady and active persistence the appointed course of the race that is set before us. Looking away [from all that will distract] to Jesus, Who is the Leader and the Source of our faith [giving the first incentive for our belief] and is also its Finisher [bringing it to maturity and perfection].*

James 1:3-4 *(AMP) "Be assured and understand that the trial and proving of your faith bring out endurance and steadfastness and* <u>*patience*</u>. *But let endurance and steadfastness and patience have full play and do a thorough work, so that you may be [people] perfectly and fully developed [with no defects], lacking in nothing."*

So exercise the fruit of the Spirit in your life. Stand your ground and defend what you have gained (or lost). Keep that ground, be courageous and do whatever is required – no matter how hard or difficult it may seem. Then you will develop in this wonderful gift called patience.

After working on patience I had come to a time in my weight loss journey that I didn't really *want* to continue. I wasn't sure I wanted to reach the goal I had previously set. However, there were still more lessons to be learned and another characteristic that God wanted to develop in me. It's a little thing called perseverance.

Chapter Eight

I'M NEVER GONNA MAKE IT

The day I weighed in and still had 10 pounds to goal I was standing at the scale thrilled. I quietly announced my current weight loss to those around me but when I sat down to wait for the meeting I heard these thoughts "You'll never get there. It'll take too long". "You might as well quit now". Well we all know the voice of our Shepherd and because of the Word we know His character. So I knew this was not God speaking to me. These discouraging thoughts were tempting me to quit, to "give up in the last quarter", as they say in football. By the grace of God, I had lost a total of 80 pounds and I only had 10 to go to reach the goal. Why was discouragement coming now? Why would I be tempted to quit so close to goal? During the following weeks I had yet another lesson to learn on the way to the scale.

What is that "thing" that keeps people going in the right direction against all odds? What is that "thing" that causes men to continue fighting in the War? What is that "thing" that gives a woman strength and endurance to go through with the birth of a child? What is that "thing" that Thomas Edison, Benjamin Franklin, and Abraham Lincoln all had? What is that "thing" that keeps a parent praying for their child and expecting their highest potential? That "thing", I believe, is perseverance.

Perseverance is found one time in the Bible as this word but the attitude of perseverance and persistency is found over and over. In Ephesians there is a list of armor, tools that the Holy Spirit has given us to put on before we pray. At the end of that list is this Scripture: **Ephesians 6:18 *"Praying always with all prayer and supplication in the Spirit, and watching thereunto with all perseverance and supplication for all saints."***

This word perseverance comes from the Greek word "proskarteresis" which means persistency. In Ephesians 6:18 the Holy Spirit is instructing us to stay alert and be persistent in praying for believers. <u>Vines Expository Dictionary of Biblical Words</u> says this word means to be steadfast, it denotes to continue steadfastly in a thing and give unremitting care to it.

<u>Noah Webster's Dictionary of 1828</u> defines perseverance and persistency and they are almost synonymous words. Perseverance is persistency in anything undertaken; constant in pursuit; to pursue steadily; not to give over or abandon what is undertaken.

Persistency means the same thing with the exception that persistence implies more obstinacy or stubbornness. So to persevere means to be persistent, don't give up what you started, pursue it to the end. Henry Ward Beecher once said "The difference between perseverance and obstinacy is that one comes from a strong will, and the other from a strong won't." I'd rather be on the side of "a strong will".

Another word that means perseverance in the Bible is found in **Colossians 1:11** Paul's praying that you would be ***"Strengthened with all might, according to His glorious power, unto all patience and longsuffering with joyfulness."***

This word longsuffering is the Greek word "makrothumia" which means patience, endurance, constancy, steadfastness, perseverance. What's God saying to us? Be strengthened unto perseverance or persistency. Why? Because when you begin a pursuit, whether spiritual or natural, you will need to pursue it to the end, against all obstacles, no matter what happens between A and Z, if you really want to reach your destiny and be successful.

So Close to Goal

At my heaviest I was a size 24 and when I reached a 14 I was feeling pretty good. I felt good and I felt like I looked good. I was active, had a sense of accomplishment and I really wanted to quit. Once again, I believed I had it down and could do this on my own. The only problem was – I wasn't at my weight goal. This was my fourth time joining Weight Watchers and I had never made it to goal. Even though I didn't feel like I needed to lose more at my age I wanted to get to goal and in order to do that I would have to persevere.

Too many times we begin something but then don't finish it. We give up when the going gets tough. Unlike the story of this Olympic hopeful from Tanzania that I found on the internet.

The story says that hours behind the runner in front of him, the last marathoner finally entered the Olympic stadium. By that time, the drama of the day's events was almost over and most of the spectators had gone home. This athlete's story, however, was still being played out. Limping into the arena, the Tanzanian runner grimaced with every step, his knee bleeding and bandaged from an earlier fall. His ragged appearance immediately caught the attention of the remaining crowd, who cheered him on to the finish line. Why did he stay in the race? What made him endure his injuries to the end? When asked these questions later, he replied, "My country did not send me 7,000 miles away to start the race. They sent me 7,000 miles to finish it."

If we're ever going to succeed we must finish what we start, no matter what obstacles arise.

One thing I found when learning to eat healthy

is that I was thinking about food all the time. Now believe me, I was thinking about food before I started this journey but it was in a different way. Eating our old way we're always thinking about what would taste good, or what smells good right now, or what am I craving and how fast can I get it?

When learning to eat healthy I found myself thinking about food all the time as well, but my thoughts were changing. What can I eat that will fill me up? What would give me energy? What can I get so that I get enough fruits and vegetables in my diet? What is high in fiber? What can I fix for dinner that will be healthy and still taste delicious? Do you see what I mean? Your thoughts change towards food as you persevere in choosing a healthy lifestyle.

Many times we are faced with things in the natural that teach us to persevere so we will be fit in the spiritual arena as well.

Just recently I had an opportunity to want to give up in the natural realm. Although we are used to the wind in Bullhead City where we live and pastor, I had an experience with the wind in Oklahoma while visiting my daughter and her family. We had gone to a friend's house for dinner and when Lindsay was ready to take her baby home we put on our jackets and walked outside into the winter cold and found out the wind was blowing, and it was blowing strong. Our vehicle was about 10 yards away but when I got about half way I wanted to quit. I turned around and looked at the house and it was 5 yards back, but the vehicle was 5 yards in front of me. I could choose to go back or go forward, and I was torn between the two? It was too cold to do either one but I would be a lot colder if I just stood outside in the wind. What a dilemma! Of course I chose to go forward.

The same rings true in dealing with my weight. Sitting in that folding chair in that fellowship hall, I had a choice to make. Was I going to choose to go back to my old way of eating even before I had reached the finish line? Was I going to walk out before I reached goal like I had done so many times before? Was I going to quit just 10 pounds away? Or was I going to go forward no matter how long it took me to get there?

Beware of Time Limits

I think some of our problems exist because we set a time limit for ourselves. "If I haven't lost x-amount of pounds by such-and-such date then I quit." "If I haven't seen any results by this date then I'm not praying anymore". No, God has you on a course and it's your job to finish it. You can't blame God if *you* don't persistently stick with it.

In ministry we've seen people so gun-ho on a project but when it didn't happen on their time schedule they gave up. We can't limit God, or ourselves by setting a time schedule. If you're really in faith you'll believe that God will do what He said He will do, no matter how long it takes.

Perseverance Exemplified

Aren't we glad that the sixteenth president of the United States didn't give up when everything didn't fit his time schedule? Here's a time line on President Abraham Lincoln that I found on the internet:

- 1809 Abraham Lincoln was born.
- 1816 His family was forced out of their home. He had to work to support them. He was only 7 years old at the time.
- 1818 His mother died when he was 9.
- 1831 Failed in business. He was now 22.
- 1832 Ran for state legislature - lost.
- 1832 Also lost his job - wanted to go to law school but couldn't get accepted.
- 1833 Borrowed some money from a friend to begin a business and by the end of the year he was bankrupt. He spent the next 17 years of his life paying off this debt.
- 1834 Ran for state legislature again - won.
- 1835 Was engaged to be married, sweetheart died and his heart was broken.
- 1836 Had a total nervous breakdown and was in bed for six months.
- 1838 Sought to become speaker of the state legislature - defeated.

- 1840 Sought to become elector - defeated.
- 1843 Ran for Congress - lost.
- 1846 Ran for Congress again - this time he won went to Washington and did a good job.
- 1848 Ran for re-election to Congress - lost.
- 1849 Sought the job of land officer in his home state - rejected.
- 1854 Ran for Senate of the United States - lost.
- 1856 Sought the Vice-Presidential nomination at his party's national convention - got less than 100 votes.
- 1858 Ran for U.S. Senate again - again he lost.
- 1860 Elected president of the United States at the age of 51.

President Abraham Lincoln had many opportunities to quit - but he didn't and because he didn't quit, he became one of the greatest presidents in the history of our country.

In letters to other people he made statements like:

> "My path was worn and slippery. My foot slipped from under me, knocking the other out of the way, but I recovered and said to myself 'It's a slip and not a fall'."

> "The fight must go on. The cause of civil

liberty must not be surrendered at the end of one, or even one hundred defeats."
--From the November 19, 1858 Letter to Henry Asbury

"I know not how to aid you, save in the assurance of one of mature age, and much severe experience, that you can not fail, if you resolutely determine, that you will not."
--From the July 22, 1860 Letter to George Latham

The perseverance exemplified by this man is extraordinary but should it be? Should it not be normal for us to persevere in any undertaking that we embrace? Shouldn't it be abnormal if at any time we give up on something? Giving up! Now *that* should be out of the ordinary. Because we are born of God we should be people of perseverance. If we were, our marriages would last a lifetime, our families would be closer and our employers would be giving *us* the promotions.

I had an Instructor in Bible School that had shared with us a story of perseverance. Back in the 50's God had told him to have a tent revival in a certain town. He set everything up, advertised, and when it came time to start the meetings no one was there but his wife. He looked at his wife and said "Honey, go to the organ". She looked around and said "no one's here". He said "That doesn't matter, God said to have a tent-revival so we're going to have a tent revival." This went on for several days and then one person came in, met Jesus, was saved and healed instantly. The next night the tent was full of people and there is still a church there today because of his obedience and perseverance.

Don't Give Up

How many of us can look back over our lives and see areas where we gave up too quickly when we should have persevered? Although we can't go back we *can* learn from our mistakes and go forward. It's always too soon to quit and now is definitely not the time to quit on your faith because Jesus is coming soon.

In **John 14:1-3** Jesus promised that He will come again. **John 14:1-3** *"Let not your heart be troubled: ye believe in God, believe also in me. In my Father's house are many mansions: if it were not so, I would have told you. I go to prepare a place for you. And if I go and prepare a place for you, <u>I will come again</u>, and receive you unto myself; that where I am, there ye may be also."*

As soon as Jesus left this earth there was a promise that He would return. Look at **Acts 1:8-11** *(NLT)* says *"But when the Holy Spirit has come upon you, you will receive power and will tell people about me everywhere — in Jerusalem, throughout Judea, in Samaria, and to the ends of the earth." It was not long after He said this that He was taken* *up into the sky while they were watching, and He disappeared into a cloud. As they were straining their eyes to see Him, two white-robed men suddenly stood there among them. They said, "Men of Galilee, why are you standing here staring at the sky? Jesus has been taken away from you into heaven. And someday, just as you saw Him go, <u>He will return</u>!"*

Jesus said to us in **Revelation 3:11** *(AMP)* *"<u>I am coming quickly</u>; hold fast what you have, so that no one may rob you and deprive you of your crown."*

You can see Biblical prophecy unfolding daily. As we watch the signs of the times you will also see people giving up for four main reasons. I hope I can encourage you to not be one of those that throw in the towel right before Jesus raptures the church. The four things to watch out for are:

The first reason people will give up in the last days is due to false teaching. **I Timothy 4:1** warns us *"Now the Spirit speaketh expressly, that in the latter times some shall depart from the faith, giving heed to seducing spirits, and doctrines of devils". The New Living Translation puts it this way, "Now the Holy Spirit tells us clearly that in the last times some will turn away from what we believe; they will follow lying spirits and teachings that come from demons."*

The Greek word for seduce is "planao" which

means "to cause to wander, lead astray", to deceive or corrupt, to cause one to stray from the Truth. You will see some depart from the faith because they have been led away by false teaching, better known as "new age" but in reality are simply old lies. You've seen it already. Many have left the church because they didn't want to be challenged to change. They want an easy Gospel, they don't want to hear about sacrifice so they follow seducing spirits that lead them away from Jesus.

The second reason people will quit in the last days is because they simply disobey their conscience. **1 Timothy 1:19-20 *(NLT)* says *"Cling tightly to your faith in Christ, and always keep your conscience clear. For some people have deliberately violated their consciences; as a result, their faith has been shipwrecked."***

If you don't cling tightly to your faith in Jesus it will be easy to violate your conscience. And if you refuse to listen to your conscience you will shipwreck your faith. One way to follow the Holy Spirit is to follow your conscience, that's if you have renewed your mind to the Word of God.

Thirdly, persecution is another reason people will give up on their faith. **Mt 24:9-14 *(NLT)* says *"Then you will be arrested, persecuted, and killed. You will be hated all over the world because of your allegiance to me. And many will turn away from me and betray and hate each other. And many false*** *prophets will appear and will lead many people astray. Sin will be rampant everywhere, and the love of many will grow cold. But those who endure to the end will be saved. And the Good News about the Kingdom will be preached throughout the whole world, so that all nations will hear it; and then, finally, the end will come.*

I urge you to not give up just because you are hated for your faith in Jesus Christ. Endure to the end because your end is way better than your beginning. Mark Hankins says "If you knew what was on the other side of your mountain, you'd tell it to move". Now is the time to use your authority that was given to you by Jesus Himself. Stand your ground and don't lose *any* of it. Believe me, the devil will take up the slack if there is any, so hold on tight. You win in the end.

The fourth reason that I have found why people will leave their faith in the last days is because of the love of the world. **II Timothy 4:9-10** *says "Make every effort to come to me soon. For Demas has deserted me for <u>love of this present world</u> and has gone to Thessalonica; Crescens [has gone] to Galatia, Titus to Dalmatia."*

Demas was Paul's co-worker in the ministry (Philemon 24). But the Scripture tells us that he deserted the faith for love of this present world. He loved the world more than God and so he quit.

In Genesis chapter 19 God told Lot and his wife

not to look back. He's pleading with us to not desire the things of the world – your old life, because it is not comparable to eternal life and abundant life that He has prepared for us.

In I Samuel chapter 30 David got discouraged because the Amalekites had taken everything from them. In fact, his own people talked of stoning him. But David encouraged himself in the Lord, persevered, and inquired of the Lord. The Lord was faithful, as usual, and gave him the steps to recover all, and David did just as the Lord said, he recovered it all.

You Can Reach Your Goals

I encourage you to persevere, don't quit and don't give up. You really can reach your weight goals and any other goals that you may want to accomplish. Do like David did and inquire of the Lord. Then break down your goals in to reachable aspirations. Then you will be able to persevere without much difficulty.

When I first began my journey of health I could not believe that I would be at the size I am today. I wanted to, but I couldn't get my faith there until I persevered closer to reaching my goal.

Perseverance and persistency is the hardest when you're facing defeat. There are things that come up that seem like it's gonna bring defeat. For instance, when you've been invited out to eat with someone that could care less what they eat, let alone what you eat, it's the night before weigh in but you know you should spend time with this person. What do you do? Do you give up and say "Oh well, there goes that weeks weight loss". Should you not go with them? Or should you go and find the healthiest thing on the menu no matter how good the high-caloric food smells? Only *you* can answer that question for yourself. But for me, I had to persevere in my weight-loss journey and the choice is always mine. However, you *can* do both.

If the devil can get you to quit at the last moment, he'll steal your miracle. Even in writing this book I had to put it on the back shelf to take care of some church business at the beginning of the year. I was tempted several times to forget about the book but I had already been learning about persistency and perseverance. Nothing and no one was going to get me to quit and give up. God had instructed me to put these lessons in writing and even if no one reads it, I've finished what I started.

Some of you may be reading this book saying "so what if I give up, I don't think I'll ever reach my goal anyway". Well, where would we be today if Thomas Edison had not persevered? He has said "I never failed once. It just happened to be a 2000-step process." How many steps to your goal have you taken? Are you not successful if you get up one more time than you fall?

If you are ever going to succeed at losing weight,

or anything else worthwhile, you must continue to persevere. The Bible says:

"For a righteous man falls seven times,

and rises again." (Proverbs 24:16).

So if you have not reached your goal yet, keep persevering. You're closer than you were yesterday.

Chapter Nine

INFECTIOUS HEALTH

More often than not, when we hear the word "infectious" we associate it with sickness and disease. After all, this word is defined in the online dictionary as "communicable by infection, as from one person to another or from one part of the body to another". Wordnet defined it as "easily spread".

But what are we saying when we say "Infectious Health"? Let's first look at this word "health", and then we'll examine how a body works.

Jesus Provided Healing for Us

Let's dive into the Scripture for a moment and look at the Healer of disease. When Jesus told His disciples that He was going to go away and send the comforter He said in **John 16:7 (AMP) *"However, I am telling you nothing but the truth when I say it is profitable (good, expedient, advantageous) for you that I go away…"*.** Did you know that Jesus' going away could not be profitable, or to our advantage, if His going away would withdraw the manifestation of His compassion to heal the sick, or even modify it in any degree?

No, emphatically no*! Jesus is the same yesterday, today and forever. (Hebrews 11:8). He is Jehovah Rapha, the Lord that heals you (Exodus 15:2),* and His plan is for you to be healed and live in divine health. **Matthew 8:16-17** *says "When the evening was come, they brought unto Him many that were possessed with devils: and He cast out the spirits with His word, and healed all that were sick: That it might be fulfilled which was spoken by Isaiah the prophet, saying, Himself took <u>our</u> infirmities, and bare <u>our</u> sicknesses."* You'd have to misquote that verse to leave yourself out of it.

What Scripture in Isaiah was Jesus referring to? Look at **Isaiah 53:4-5** *"Surely He hath borne our griefs, and carried our sorrows: yet we did esteem Him stricken, smitten of God, and afflicted. But He was wounded for our transgressions, He was bruised for our iniquities: the chastisement of our peace was upon Him; and with His stripes we are healed."*

The word "borne" is the Hebrew word "nasa" which means to lift off. Jesus lifted our sickness off of us. How do we know it was sickness and not just grief? Because the Hebrew word for "griefs" is the word "choli" which means sickness and disease.

And every other place in the Bible this word is translated sickness and disease.

Then come over to the New Testament to **I Peter 2:24** and He says *"...by Whose stripes you were healed".* We WERE healed. When? When Jesus took the stripes, the beating, upon His back for you and me.

Sometimes people wonder if its God's will for them to be healed. Well, first of all, Jesus said it was when the leper asked Him that same question in Matthew 8. Secondly, in **Acts 10:38**, and many other Scriptures tell us the same thing, that *"Jesus went about doing good, and healing all that were oppressed of the devil."* And then we find out in **Hebrews 1:13** *that Jesus is the express image of the Father.* We also see in **John 8:29** that Jesus said *"And He that sent me is with me: the Father hath not left me alone; for I do always those things that <u>please</u> Him."*

Well If Jesus only did what pleased the Father, then Jesus must have been doing the will of God when He was healing all that were sick and it must have pleased the Father.

I know there are people that don't understand healing and haven't received the manifestation of their healing. But it doesn't mean it's not God's will to heal you. According to Scripture – it is! So I encourage you to dig into the Scripture to find out what God says about it. But now let's take a look at infection.

How Does Infection Spread?

What happens to other parts of your body when one bodily part hurts? How do infections spread from one part of the body to the next? We must understand how the body functions to understand how the Body of Christ functions.

Most people have experienced an infection in their body at one time or another in their life. Infections can start many ways but one way that is common is when an infected person comes in contact with another person. It can be airborne, by touching a person, or simply by touching something the infected person has touched.

Now, we understand we've been redeemed from sickness and disease, but for the sake of discussion let's see how infection *could* spread.

An infected person walks in the grocery store and everything they touch is touched with that infection. Some items that they touch they put in their basket and other items they touch they put back on the shelf. The money they give the clerk is touched by this infection and that money goes into the cash register where it touches the other money. Now that money is given to you. You have put some of the touched items into your basket and some of the monetary change you received was touched by the infected person. You take it home and others in your home touch those items that have been touched by infection.

If it were not for the way God created this incredible body to fight and ward off infections with our immune system, and for the stripes that Jesus took on His back for our healing, we would be sick all the time. But *"...we are fearfully and wonderfully made...". (Psalm 139:14).* The purpose of the last paragraph is to show you how infections can touch people that you don't even know. So it is true in the Body of Christ.

How Does the Body of Christ Function?

Once you are born again you are born into the family of God and another name used for that family is "Body of Christ". We function as a body and we all have different jobs accordingly as the Spirit has gifted us in the body. Take a look at how the Holy Spirit described the function of the "Body":

> **I Corinthians 12:12-27. *(NLT)*** *"The human body has many parts, but the many parts make up only one body. So it is with the body of Christ. Some of us are Jews, some are Gentiles, some are slaves, and some are free. But we have all been baptized into Christ's body by one Spirit, and we have all received the same Spirit. Yes, the body has many different parts, not just one part. If the foot says, "I am not a part of the body because I am not a hand," that does not make it any less a part of the body. And if the ear says, "I am not part of the body because I am only an ear and not an eye," would that*

make it any less a part of the body? Suppose the whole body were an eye — then how would you hear? Or if your whole body were just one big ear, how could you smell anything? But God made our bodies with many parts, and He has put each part just where He wants it. What a strange thing a body would be if it had only one part! Yes, there are many parts, but only one body. The eye can never say to the hand, "I don't need you." The head can't say to the feet, "I don't need you." In fact, some of the parts that seem weakest and least important are really the most necessary. And the parts we regard as less honorable are those we clothe with the greatest care. So we carefully protect from the eyes of others those parts that should not be seen, while other parts do not require this special care. So God has put the body together in such a way that extra honor and care are given to those parts that have less dignity. This makes for harmony among the members, so that all the members care for each other equally. If one part suffers, all the parts suffer with it, and if one part is honored, all the parts are glad. Now all of you together are Christ's body, and each one of you is a separate and necessary part of it."

Did you see that? We are all a necessary part of the Body and what you do affects others in the Body. You cannot be a foot and say "Where I go is none of your business Mr. Eye", because where you go will affect the eye every time. Along the same line of thought being part of a body is very beneficial. When your arm is wounded the rest of your body will rush to the aid of that arm for healing and restoration because it is needed.

One of the reasons why some people don't want to go to church is because they don't want to be accountable to others in the Body. But the truth is, if they stay dismembered from the rest of the Body very long, they will die. Just as any part of the physical body cannot live without the other parts of the body very long. It must be connected to the body to live. Isn't it wonderful how Jesus, Who instituted the Church, designed it so we would need one another?

I'm not suggesting that it's always easy to get along with everyone else. We've all been raised so differently and we have values that differ from one another although once born again your values change to line up with the Word of God. But the Bible says *"Iron sharpens irons, so a man sharpeneth the countenance of his friend"*. **(Proverbs 27:17*)*.

Walter Martinez talks about this iron sharpening iron in his book <u>Building Better Relationships.</u>

> The word iron is in reference to an iron implement or tool, like an ax head or sword. This sharpening is done by natural means on a regular basis. You cannot wait until the tool is dull to sharpen it because you will lose productivity. Even though the sharpening process is what irritates the flesh

we must go through this process by natural means on a regular basis if we intend to stay productive in the Body of Christ. (Martinez: page 100)

So go ahead brothers and sisters, be infectious with your love as you receive sharpening from one another encouraging each other in the Lord. May this encouragement spread from one to another and to another as we work together to build His Kingdom.

Now Back to Infectious Health

When I speak of infectious health I'm speaking of 'health and fitness' as something that is easily spread. Notice infections are easily spread. Infectious health is not a difficult thing, when you receive encouragement from another person. But how is that encouragement given and how is it received?

Sometimes I've seen spouses trying to encourage their 'love' to lose weight. Not because they don't love them the way they are but because they love them so much they want them to be around for a lifetime. I know one husband that said he wanted his wife to lose weight because he saw what the extra weight was doing to his wife emotionally, and he loves her.

On the other hand, the spouse receiving the encouragement to lose weight doesn't always perceive this gift the way it's given. You must be discreet in the way that you 'help'. Sometimes the overweight spouse assumes that you are trying to control them. There are other times they think you don't love them the way they are. And if the overweight spouse thinks it's impossible to lose weight they wonder if you will ever *really* love them.

As hard as you may try, convincing them of the truth will take time and dedication. Try to ask yourself how they will hear what you are saying. You know its one thing to hear the words but "how" are they hearing it? I've seen some spouses use this Scripture out of context as well as others in the Body of Christ. They say I just "spoke the truth"! Well, the Word doesn't say it like that. The Holy Spirit said to **"Speak the Truth in Love" (Ephesians 4:15)**. If you will speak the truth IN LOVE, and at the right time, it will bring encouragement every time.

And as an encouragement, why not change *your* eating habits as well? You know it's a lot easier if your spouse doesn't have to cook one way for themselves and another way for you. It would do you good as well, to get healthier. Just because you're not overweight does not mean you're healthy. Plan activities together that move your bodies, rather than just another place to sit. There are things you can do that will help encourage your spouse during the process of losing and maintaining their weight.

My husband was a blessing to me while I was

losing weight. He determined that he would be a help and not a hindrance so we changed our eating lifestyle completely. After learning about portion control we started using lunch plates at every meal since that was enough food for one person. We share meals when we eat out and we do our best not to eat too late into the night. While I was losing weight my husband lost 21 lbs without even trying. That was just with the simple changes we made together. At the writing of this book he has now lost over 60 pounds himself. Praise the Lord!

Another Way of Encouragement

Another way encouragement is given is by observation. When a person that is somewhat overweight observes an obese person decrease in size and weight it creates an encouraging inspiration that says "If they can do it I can do it". Nothing has to be said. Just exhibiting success causes others to believe that they can succeed as well.

Encouragement is also given by words of affirmation. Affirmation is a wonderful thing. It means to validate a person, to recognize or establish a persons worth. WOW! Isn't that what believers should be doing for one another? <u>In sending His only Son, God established the worth of every human being on this earth.</u> ***"For God so loved the world…"*** **(John 3:16a)**. In fact God calls people ***"…the precious fruit of the earth…"*** *in* **James 5:7**. We are precious to Him, all of us. In **Ephesians 2:10** the New Living Translation says *"We are His masterpiece".* The Creator loves His creation.

We alluded to a Scripture in **Psalm 139:14** but let's go back there to see how much God thinks of us:

> **Psalm 139:1-18** *"O LORD, You have examined my heart and know everything about me. You know when I sit down or stand up. You know my every thought when far away. You chart the path ahead of me and tell me where to stop and rest. Every moment You know where I am. You know what I am going to say even before I say it, LORD. You both precede and follow me. You place your hand of blessing on my head. Such knowledge is too wonderful for me, too great for me to know! I can never escape from Your spirit! I can never get away from Your presence! …You made all the delicate, inner parts of my body and knit me together in my mother's womb. Thank you for making me so wonderfully complex! Your workmanship is marvelous — and how well I know it. You watched me as I was being formed in utter seclusion, as I was woven together in the dark of the womb. You saw me before I was born. Every day of my life was recorded in your book. Every moment was laid out before a single day had passed. <u>How precious are your thoughts about me, O God! They are innumerable! I can't even count them; they outnumber the</u>*

<u>grains of sand!</u> And when I wake up in the morning, You are still with me!"

Isn't that awesome? Jesus thinks about you – a lot! In fact, His thoughts toward you out number the grains of sand. That's unthinkable! Isn't His love amazing?

If Jesus affirms us, and He already knows everything about us, then shouldn't we be able to affirm one another? Shouldn't we validate one another's worth and the importance of the dreams that God has given them? Shouldn't we accept and affirm the gifts that were given each individual by the grace of God? The Holy Spirit instructs us to do so in the following verses as well as throughout Scripture: **Heb 10:24** *NLT* *"Think of ways to encourage one another to outbursts of love and good deeds"*. **1 Thessalonians 5:11 NLT** *"So encourage each other and build each other up"*.

The night I achieved my weight goal my leader told me that *I* was the inspiration. I didn't start this journey to inspire others to lose weight, I started this journey because *I* needed to lose weight. But in the process others were being inspired by my success and I have found that each person's individual success since then – has inspired still many more.

In fact, this chapter is titled 'Infectious Health' because of something one of our youth leaders (and a very dear friend) said to me. "You should have a title in your book called Infectious Health". I asked him why and he made this statement "Once you began to get healthy then others in church got inspired to get healthy as well. In fact, when they began to show signs that they were getting healthy they inspired others and it spread not only through our church but through places that we work and in our families. This health was infectious".

At the beginning I was so busy working on me that I didn't even notice that I had been encouraging others in my circle of influence. I had decided that I was going to do this no matter what anyone else said or did but I began to watch and listen. I ran into other people that had seen me from a distance and they asked others what I was doing to lose weight. They later came to me and told me that I had inspired them to lose weight and yet I hadn't even talked to them. That's infectious health, and that's encouragement. But know this, whatever way it comes; <u>encouragement can cause a seemingly defeated person to fight for success</u>, much like this fictional story of frogs that I'd like to share with you:

> There was a group of frogs who were traveling through the woods, and two of them fell into a deep pit. When the other frogs saw how deep the pit was, they told the two frogs that they were as good as dead. The two frogs ignored the comments and tried to jump up out of the pit with all their might. The other frogs kept telling them to stop, that they were as good as dead. Finally, one of the

frogs took heed to what the other frogs were saying and gave up. He fell down and died. The other frog continued to jump as hard as he could. Once again, the crowd of frogs yelled at him to stop the pain and just die. He jumped even harder and finally made it out. When he got out, the other frogs said, "Did you not hear us?" The frog explained "I'm sorry, I'm deaf! I thought you were encouraging me the whole time".

What could we accomplish if we thought others were encouraging us? What would we be bold enough to do if we thought the limits would be endless? How many of us have ever had a dream? Did we lose that dream due to discouragement? Have we assumed "If I had lived somewhere else", "If I had gone to a different college", "If I had had the money to attend that college", "If I had had a strong family that pushed me more", "If I hadn't got married so young", "If I hadn't had children so young", "If I had had more time", "If I were older", "If I were younger", "If I lived in a different place". There is excuse after excuse but none of them really hold up because we always have the opportunity to encourage ourselves if no one else does.

There's a true story in I Samuel chapter 30 that we alluded to in an earlier chapter but it would be helpful for you to remember:

David and his men returned home to Ziklag

to find that the Amalekites had burned Ziklag to the ground and carried off the women and children. When David and his men saw the ruins and realized what had happened to their families, they cried in desperation. David was now in serious trouble because his men were bitter about losing their wives and children, and they began to talk of stoning him. But <u>David encouraged himself in the LORD his God</u>.

And David inquired of the Lord. And the LORD told him, ***"Go after them. You will surely recover everything that was taken from you!"*** So David and men set out, fought the enemy and got back everything the Amalekites had taken. Nothing was missing: small or great, son or daughter, nor anything else that had been taken. David brought everything back.

When you get discouraged and there is no one to encourage you. Or it seems no one is encouraging you, then *you* encourage yourself in the Lord. Begin to say about you what God says about you.

***"I will succeed at this because God <u>always</u> causes me to triumph in Christ"*. II Corinthians 2:14**

***"I can do all things through Christ that strengthens me"*. Philippians 3:14**

"The Lord is the strength of my life, of whom shall I be afraid". **Psalm 27:1**

"When I am weak God gives me power and He increases strength to me when I have no might" **Isaiah 40:29**

"Let the weak say I am strong" **Joel 3:10**

"I am His workmanship, His masterpiece, a beautiful thing." **Ephesians 2:10**

Criticism is poisonous

Infectious criticism can be poisonous. I have often wondered why some people have trouble encouraging others. We've all known them. If anything is going good they'll point out the bad. If you're trying to do something right, they'll make sure to show you where you're wrong. Whatever you say will go under their personal microscope and you'll hear from them in a few days with all the corrections *you* need to make. The Word says in **Romans 14:3-4 (NLT):** *"Who are you to condemn God's servants? They are responsible to the Lord, so let Him tell them whether they are right or wrong. The Lord's power will help them do as they should."*

Do we not think that God is capable of correcting His children on His own? Or do we think that He has given *us* the assignment to be judge and jury? The Bible says in **Proverbs 3:12 (AMP)** *For whom the Lord loves He corrects, even as a father corrects the son in whom he delights."*

What would we accomplish if we thought no one would criticize our next endeavor? Now staying within the boundaries of the will and Word of God, of course – what would you accomplish within the next five years if you had encouragement to do so?

After tasting success and encouragement during my weight loss journey I have earned my Masters in Theology, written this book, AND got it published. I've also written a few other things that I may publish as well if the Lord directs me to. Let me tell you, <u>encouragement breeds accomplishment, but criticism breeds failure.</u>

Be careful what you say to others because it is seed sown and it will come back to you. What you sow, you will reap. What goes around comes around. For every kick, there's a kickback. In fact the Word says it like this in **Matt 7:1-2 *AMP: "DO NOT judge and criticize and condemn others, so that you may not be judged and criticized and condemned yourselves. For just as you judge and criticize and condemn others, you will be judged and criticized and condemned, and in accordance with the measure you [use to] deal out to others, it will be dealt out again to you."***

Constructive criticism

Now there is such a thing as constructive criticism so we mustn't wear our feelings on our shoulders causing others to walk on eggshells around us. If there is something to be learned we need to learn it. If there is a correction to be made we need to correct it. If we don't allow anyone to speak into our lives we may just remain in the mess we're in. Constructive criticism will help build us spiritually and physically as well.

If I really did know how to control my eating then I would not have needed a weekly meeting or a leader that would give me some constructive criticism. I needed some correction so that I could begin to go down the right path to health and fitness and succeed in my weight loss goals.

The key is to not get offended when someone offers constructive criticism. Offense is a trap of the enemy and if you yield to it you will get ensnared every time. So ask yourself questions when someone tells you the truth in love. Ask yourself if any part of that statement was true. If so, heed to the truth and thank them for pointing it out to you so you can grow. If it's not true maybe you can give that person an explanation so they have some understanding of what's really going on. This will be an opportunity for *them* to receive some constructive criticism. But please do all things in love. Most importantly, DON'T GET OFFENDED!

It could also be that what they said to you is true and you're not ready to receive it yet. It might take years before you really yield to it. But when you do, thank the Lord for His mercy and go on with God.

As you do these things and love one another you'll see that you will be part of a growing Body of Christ. It is vitally important that we encourage one another to be healthy. So go ahead brother and sister – BE INFECTIOUS WITH YOUR HEALTH!

CONCLUSION

"ARE WE THERE YET?"

"Are we there yet?" You've either said this yourself or you've had children that made this statement while traveling, and sometimes the distance was not so far. As impatient and predictable children can be while traveling we prove to be the same when we are working on changes in different areas of our lives, especially when pursuing a healthy lifestyle. Sometimes the distance from weight "a" to weight "z" is not so far, but impatience will make it seem like a lifetime.

The night I went to weigh in to see if I had reached goal I felt like that little child again asking, "Are we there yet?" As I put one foot on, and then another, the scale read my weight. My husband had gone with me to rejoice in my victory and once again I was uncertain if I had reached my goal. I had only one pound to lose that week and I was still wondering if that last pound was gone. It was customary for me, and most people I know, to wear the same clothes every week to weigh in and remove all jewelry and shoes. I stepped on the electronic scale and my husband stepped behind my leader to see the scale monitor. My leader was just as excited as I was and with great anticipation I heard the words "you did it, you've reached your goal!" I felt a big cool-aid smile come across my face as I looked up at my husband giving me a kiss. Then I looked down at my leader with tears in my eyes and softly said "thank you". She stood as tall as her little frame would stand and gave me a big hug telling me that I was the one that did it. She said "You were the inspiration". But I knew what the truth was. The grace of God alone carried me through this. Jesus is the one that led me to Weight Watchers, to sit under the direction of this wonderful little leader, and it was by His grace that I was standing here, at goal.

I knew I hadn't accomplished this on my own because ***<u>God</u> always causes me to triumph in Christ Jesus" (II Corinthians 2:14).*** If it weren't for the help of the Holy Spirit I would not have walked away from pride, fear, sickness, and impatience. I never would have learned these lessons that He had taught me over the passed year and four months.

At the finishing of this book I have now lost 105 pounds. I reached my goal, passed it a little and maintained for six weeks. I have become not only a free lifetime member in Weight Watchers but I currently work for them as a leader. However, the lectures are not my main source of encouragement, Jesus is. Many times I lie in my bed and say, "Jesus, thank you for helping me with this. It really has meant a lot to me". Jesus really is the strength of my life. As I said at the beginning of this book, I've tried to lose weight many times and many different ways before – but this time I repented of pride, responded to God's grace and found His grace is sufficient for me!

Even after all the weight is gone, and even though I certainly love helping others through their weight loss journey, my goal is not to be a leader but a mirror. **II Corinthians 3:16-18** *says "…whenever anyone turns to the Lord, then the veil is taken away. Now, the Lord is the Spirit, and wherever the Spirit of the Lord is, He gives freedom. And all of us have had that veil removed so that <u>we can be mirrors that brightly reflects the glory of the Lord</u>. And as the Spirit of the Lord works within us, we become more and more like Him and reflect His glory even more"*.

I want to be a mirror that reflects Jesus to others. I want people to look clearly in to my life and not see a distorted view of Jesus but to see Him just as He is. If you can see Jesus you can respond to Him. He's the one that gave His life for you. He's the one that is the good Shepherd. He's the one that loves you with an everlasting love. And He's the One that is the strength of your life.

Respond to Him – respond to His grace because the journey you are on is not greater than His grace!

BIBLIOGRAPHY

Renner, Rick; Sparkling Gems of the Greek, Teach All Nations. Tulsa, OK

Hankins, Mark; The Power of Identification with Christ, MHM Publications. Alexandria, LA

Thompson, Robb. Excellence of Character, Tintley Park, IL. Family Harvest Church

Martinez, Walter. Building Better Relationship, Phoenix, AZ. Redeemed Christian Center

Backus, William. Telling Yourself the Truth, Minneapolis, MN. Bethany House Publishers

Thayer's Greek Lexicon, Electronic Database. Copyright © 2000, 2003 by Biblesoft, Inc.

Biblesoft's New Exhaustive Strong's Numbers and Concordance with Expanded Greek-Hebrew Dictionary. Copyright © 1994, 2003 Biblesoft, Inc. and International Bible Translators, Inc

Scripture quotations that are not marked are taken from:

- The King James Version of the Holy Bible

Other Biblical quotations are taken from:

- NAS are taken from the New American Standard Version
- AMP from the Amplified Bible
- NLT from the New Living Translation
- TLB from The Living Bible
- NIV from the New International Version.

Barbara Odom is married, has two married daughters and four grandchildren. She co-pastors with her husband Tim at Spirit Life Foursquare Church in Bullhead City, Arizona, where she oversees the Christian Education of their members from the youngest to the oldest.

She is an alumnus of Rhema Bible Training Center and has earned her Masters of Theology from Life Christian University. She is licensed and ordained with the International Church of the Foursquare Gospel and is a regularly invited speaker at other churches and women's events.

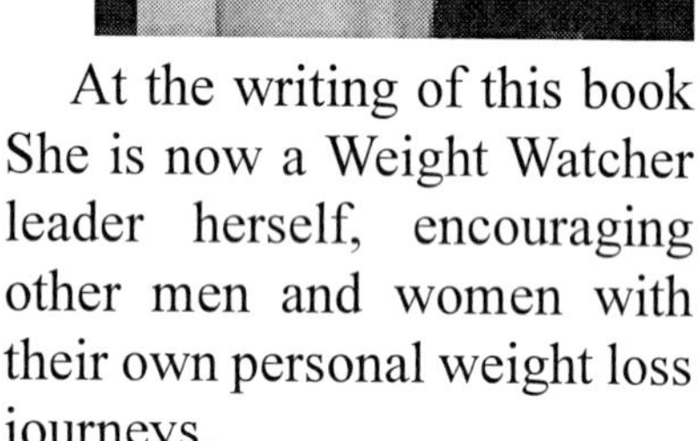

At the writing of this book She is now a Weight Watcher leader herself, encouraging other men and women with their own personal weight loss journeys.

Her hopes are not that you will go out and join the weight loss program that the Lord led her to, but rather that you will be encour-

aged to allow the Lord to reveal and heal areas in your heart that when mended, will bring an outward metamorphosis of an inward transformation. The first step through this process is being honest with God and with yourself.

Contact Information

If you would like more
information on other materials
by Barbara Odom,
please contact us.

Web site:
www.spiritlifebhc.org

Phone:
928.542.9558

Mailing Address:
Spirit Life Church
2850 Silver Creek Rd.
Bullhead City, AZ 86442
Attn: Pastor Barbara Odom